CLIFFHANGERS

CLIFFHANGERS

SPIRITUAL GROWTH THROUGH UNPOPULAR CHOICES

Dr. Felecia Rodgers

authorHOUSE®

AuthorHouse™
1663 Liberty Drive
Bloomington, IN 47403
www.authorhouse.com
Phone: 1-800-839-8640

Published by AuthorHouse 04/25/2016

ISBN: 978-1-4918-0807-8 (sc)
ISBN: 978-1-4918-0806-1 (hc)
ISBN: 978-1-4918-0805-4 (e)

Library of Congress Control Number: 2013914605

Print information available on the last page.

This book is printed on acid-free paper.

CONTENTS

This work is dedicated to my family and the **Each One Reach One Mission** family in remembrance of every cliff experience; to Shirley, my sister in Christ, who God placed in my life at a pivotal time on the mountain. God positioned us to walk along individual paths of distress, despair, delight and disillusion uniting us through the experience of a *White Funeral* to bask in His Glorious Splendor. There on the cliff we were together as God proclaimed "keep your eyes on me" and beckoned to trust Him despite perceptions and circumstances.

And my spirit has rejoiced in God my Savior, for He has had regard for the humble state of His bond slave; for behold, from this time on all generations will count me blessed.

Luke 1:47-48

To stand at the edge of a steep cliff and look down is to experience fear. We want to get out of that situation as quickly and safely as we can. To stand securely on a mountaintop and look around us is to feel awe. We could linger there forever.

Rabbi Harold Kushner
When All You've Ever Wanted Isn't Enough

Preface

The individual called of God for specific purpose recognizes that it is an honor but is humbled by the summons and exorbitant responsibility. Then, to be uprooted from the normal lifestyle of humanity and propelled into a seemingly unorthodox pattern of living is unnerving to the natural man, although compelling to the spirit of man when God's Spirit dwells. Being called, taught, prepared and sent is the sign of apostleship. Add to this assignment that the destination is unknown and outside the capacity of human understanding, and you have what appears to be the making of calamity. Yet, you are constrained to decide: "if the Lord is God, follow Him but if Baal, then follow him" (I King 18:21). Family and friends are concerned. They wonder if there is a need for medical or psychiatric attention. At times so do you, while praying, fasting, praising, crying and begging for a sign; an answer as to what to choose . . .

The King James Version of the Word of God in the Book of Matthew chapter 6 verse 33 states, "seek ye first the kingdom of God and His righteousness; and all *these* things" of which you have need, for example, all the answers to your questions, all the solutions to your problems or the correct decisions for your choices, "will be added unto you." Some people say this Scripture means:

1. Place attention on the important goals and mundane issues like day to day concerns will work out.

2. Focus on God and the things of God rather than worldly pursuits.
3. Seek God and trust Him and become more aware of one's own decisions.

It means to seek God for the decisions. Seeking God and His righteousness reveals the right state of the heart and mind toward heavenly and earthly things, conveying symmetry with godly character. Have you heard of the trust test where an individual is instructed to fall backward believing someone will catch them? God has not devised strategies which cause His children to live unharmed, although He is our protector. He requires that we develop trust in Him. This is evident by risk-taking and discomfort as we travel mountainous regions of peril and find our way to the cliff's edge. Many times upon the cliff, God directs that we close our eyes and jump. This is irrational to the mind of natural man, much like the need for a savior and a physical resurrected body. But God is the Alpha and Omega, the Author and Finisher; and the Creator of the created man, there is "nothing impossible with Him" (Luke 1:37). Jesus said in Luke chapter nine verses 57 and 58, to those who would make the decision to follow Him; just as the Son of Man faced adversity, difficulties will be encountered in acts of faith. Confronted with this fact mankind makes excuses as we vacillate between the spiritual attraction of the Word and the physical attraction of the world. Jesus emphasizes that the Kingdom of God is foremost and its service all-encompassing, stating that "no one who puts his hand to the plow and looks back is fit for the Kingdom of God (Luke 9:62). Although the directive is acknowledged, people become concerned about the nature of the task before them and stand at the cliff starkly aware of their inadequacies. We want provisions in place, prior business handled, and every "i" dotted and "t" crossed, especially when we are sure that our instructions are from God. All the contemplation reveals a fear of failure, a fear of the future and an apprehension about the unknown. Some people are so controlled by the tyranny of uncertainty that they become completely paralyzed by concerns over the outcomes of decisions affecting the future to the point of being ineffective in the present. D. Martin Lloyd—Jones asserts that "though we believe the truth, though we have been born again" having received the Holy Spirit; and "though we are most certainly children of God, we lapse into thinking as if none of these things are true."[1] We behave like children of the world, who have never been renewed. We allow the past, present and future to dominate us. "We compare our weakness, lack of strength and knowledge with the greatness of our calling, the tremendous task before us, the powerful Spirit within us and with us;" and there we stand motionless at the edge of the cliff "as if we are but our natural selves"[2] But God states He wants us off this mountain and on to the next one. He knows the sure path for us to take (Jer.6:16). So it is necessary for us to become aware of our current path and our current circumstances to become certain of the course ahead; and by faith know and accept that there is only one way meant for us.

Cliffhangers, is a text which offers its reader opportunity for a concise look at the myriad of choices in their lives and presents a biblical foundation to assist with understanding their impact on spiritual growth and with making future decisions. Decisions of choice are the hardest because each choice offers benefit and loss. ***Cliffhangers*** answers questions like: How can I increase my faith? How does every choice I make affect my spiritual growth? How does the cliffhanger experience cause my Christian identity to mature? Why am I afraid to step out on faith? When will I know that faith has overcome my fear? ***Cliffhangers,*** is designed to inspire an increasing faith in Christians as one advances toward key life goals. Its purpose is to enlighten and educate, Christians and non-Christians, on the importance of decisions relative to our choices and their influence on spiritual maturity. We all know that decisions have a causal effect; meaning the purpose, or end a decision is supposed to serve will occur, although it is possible that to engage in a decision or not to engage may result in unanticipated outcomes. The evidence demonstrates that the decisions people make transforms the life of the individual making the decision and many times the lives of others. Therefore, ***Cliffhangers*** *provides* insight into the importance of wise choices to manage a purposive Christian life. It is written to inform that every decision is potentially life-altering and has significance regarding spiritual awakening and development. It also affirms that to navigate in this life you must learn to believe that there is only one who can direct you. God, who created you, has the solution to every circumstance you will encounter. ***Cliffhangers,*** is a reminder that a leap of faith is required at the edge of your cliff. The Bible reports that our battle is not in the natural realm but in the spiritual realm and it contends that the various obstacles, trials and tests that we encounter are challenges which thwart or advance spirituality. The content of this book reveals the experience of the cliffhanger as a requisite for spiritual recognition, growth and development.

The definition of spirituality encompasses that which affects the soul: the mind, will and emotions, having an apparent intangible existence. It seems impossible for scholars to agree upon only one definition for spirituality. It is often used to describe the human need for meaning and value in and of life, and the desire for relationship whether consciously or subconsciously with a transcendent power. In the book, *Integrating Spirituality into Multicultural Counseling,* it is noted as "a code word for the depth dimension of human existence, a life force which infuses human beings with qualities of inspiration, creativity and interconnectedness."[3] The Greek prefix, *pneuma,* and the Latin root, *spiritus,* both mean breath which is the essence of life which is defined as spirituality. Spirituality is described as being like the wind; it is invisible, immaterial and powerful. John 3:8 says: *The wind blows where it wishes and you hear the sound of it, but do not know where it comes from and where it is going; so is everyone who is born of the Spirit.* Spirituality is notably experienced as an active and passive process. As an active process it presents as individualistic, unyielding to influence, rational, and selective. As the passive process it presents as a victim, innately conservative, gullible, anomic,* and vulnerable. It appears as an instinctive capacity and tendency to seek knowledge, love, meaning, hope, transcendence, coherence and compassion.

---

* **This word epitomizes the passive process of spirituality defined as being: unstable because of moral breakdown:** unstable because moral and social codes have been eroded or abandoned; **affected by alienation:** feeling alienated from society and disoriented by the perceived absence of a social or moral framework; and **somebody affected by alienation:** somebody who feels alienated and disoriented because of the lack of a social and moral framework. (Encarta® World English Dictionary [North American Edition] © & (P) 2009 Microsoft Corporation)

Although spirituality is not always associated with religion, it may be lived and expressed through religion characterized by beliefs, communal relationships, traditions and rituals. Development and growth of individual spirituality is affected as Believers proceed along the mountain road by faith, through the power of the Holy Spirit. People must travel these roads sometimes without having a clear vision of specific objectives or outcomes. Faith must be guided by the compass of God's Word to avoid myths and superficialities. We must travail through commitment and persistence which are significant aspects of faith to confidently claim the promises of God. Faith does not produce spiritual development and growth; it places the Believer where change can occur. The journey leads to the pivotal moment of decision on the cliff's edge with its potential to reconstruct the Believer's spirituality and transport them before God to be recreated into the image of Jesus Christ. Therefore, like Jesus, a Christian is no longer living in one's own strength, knowledge and wisdom, but the power of God in Christ lives through the Believer under the governance of the Holy Spirit (Gal.2:20).

As we travel along the highways of life, ascending the mountains of choice, we learn that the stated concept "all roads lead the same way" is not true. Some roads lead to dead ends, some to places you are prohibited to go, others, where you are warned you should not go and still others lead to where you wish you had not gone (Jer.18:15). Most people utilize every human effort in their attempt to make the best decision. These individuals often stand at the crest of the mountain looking for signs, miracles and wonders; trying to make sure that things will be all right based on some perceived idea; usually an idealized or glamorized concept. Some people consider their choices from a single-minded perspective without imagining the varying concepts and their consequences. Oftentimes people make impulsive decisions without being mindful of the detriment of this action. Decisions, whether circumstantial or impulsive, as well as indecision have a profound effect on spiritual engagement. ***Cliffhangers,*** is about having to make unpopular, uneasy decisions, where the results can be positive towards spiritual certainty, acknowledgement, establishment and maturity. Or negative, expressed as antagonism and demonstrated as the negation of anything spiritual; maintaining the position of self-reliance, fate or luck as it pertains to events. This text is not meant to reference decisions regarding where to go for dinner, which fork to use or what clothes to put on, but is proposed that one take an in-depth look at those decisions which can have a profound impact on your life that are often to be distinguished between many options. Therefore, the intended audience is anyone struggling with the complexity of life choices or in need of guidance with a life changing decision. It is for the individual who does not comprehend that they are in a situation of consequence or why they are even involved in the dilemma. Each one of us will find ourselves hanging around the edge of a cliff, often deemed unrelated to one's phase of life, having to make a life-changing decision just before a future day dawns.

Why is it called ***Cliffhangers***? A cliffhanger is a term used for an exaggerated narrative which concludes during a suspenseful moment, averting the progression and leaving the audience wanting to know what is going to happen next. Usually, the main character or plot is literally left hanging, in a dramatic fashion, until the story resumes which is the enticement for spectators. The term is fittingly applied to any situation or event in which the outcome remains undetermined until the last moment possible. Still, in real life the outcome is generally uncertain even after the resumption of the narrative. In ***Cliffhangers***, examples are offered from the Scriptures of individuals experiencing time at the pinnacle of the mountain, the questions they may have pondered and the outcome of their allotted time on the cliff. Why is this important? It is important to know that every choice results in decisions which affect eternal security, because God's Word articulates that it is important, and because knowing will encourage you to focus on every choice by seeking God for the decision (Prov. 3:5-6). Knowing awakens you to develop a sincere and unyielding attitude regarding your relationship to God; it places this natural life and all things related to it into proper perspective enabling you to stay on the right path in the purposes of God because we all need to learn when to be still and listen to what "thus saith the Lord" (II Tim. 4:7). Although every occasion for decision can be a cliffhanger, usually one finds that during times of life's uncertainty while seeking understanding we are standing at the edge of the cliff looking over into what appears to be nothingness without a parachute, rope or wings.

The cliff is an inevitable situation. But, if we are required to leave the cliff to develop spiritually, why do we stay on the cliff? As we live out life choosing for ourselves, we create our existence with all of its pros and cons. We only get one chance at this life which is confirmed in three forms of existence; the physical (body), platonic (soul) and autonomic (spirit). For explanation purposes, the physical is distinguishable as an identity which is unshared by any other individual. Human beings have physical features that are not obviously apparent that make them distinctive from one another. These include DNA, fingerprints, the shape of the teeth and the pattern of blood vessels in the back of the human eye that has an exclusive pattern in each person. Even with the advancements in science, these physical characteristics cannot be duplicated to become anyone else. The platonic or soul of mankind consisting of the mind, will and emotions is the sphere of idea formulation and processing. The acceptance of God, the faithful expression of this belief and the inconsistencies of love as emotion, reason as intellect and prerogative as power are evident in the human soul. The spiritual (spirit) is conceptually removed from the physical, interrelated with the platonic yet autonomic. Within the realm of the spirit, involuntary or spontaneous responses to choices are heightened and determined relevant to an individual's intrinsic and extrinsic qualities. All of this is written to emphasize that each person has been uniquely created by God (Ps. 139:13-14; Eph. 2:10). Often we take much of it for granted. On the mountain peak of revelation, we haphazardly make decisions or we take everything seriously and extract burdensome circumstances or we live life in the middle, trying to stay within a range of perceived satisfaction; *trying to get it right*, all of which end with us standing at the cliff. Many are petitioned to let go of fear and discover their faith. Whether we are aware or not, all choices lead to a place of decision and all circumstances following each decision can be associated with advancement, neutrality or even decline in spiritual growth.

I pray this book will bless many who are perched upon the cliff. DECIDE as God is calling you higher in Him through Jesus Christ, our Savior and Lord.

How long will you waiver between two opinions?

(I Kings 18:21)

Chapter One

Introduction: An appeal to Spiritual Growth

You have heard it said that if God is calling an individual to do something, then it will be easy because God will supply everything that is needed. It is no secret that He promises to supply every need, according to His riches in glory, that He will never leave nor forsake His children and since God is not a man He keeps His promises (Phil. 4:9; Heb. 13:5; Num. 23:19). However, imagine this call on your life is like coming to the edge of a mountain that you have climbed. Here on the mountain's peak, faith is challenged and you are compelled to take an initial step, make a decisive action, venture into uncertain territory or execute an unaccepted, ill-advised or unpopular choice by world standards. What happens then, when faced with an apparent setback, when a bad accident happens or disease ravages our bodies? It is most definitely not easy. Here again, our love of God is challenged and our faith is provoked. We find ourselves on a cliff. We stand confused, lonely, anguished and angry. As a child of God, we become overwhelmed with guilt for these emotions and seek God's Word for restitution. Reservation is often laid aside by the groaning of the Holy Spirit in the heart. We are summoned to a more profound relationship with God and challenged to make hard decisions. The perplexity of the cliffhanger causes one to seek solace and solutions in the midst of randomness and unpredictability. The Bible says that the Word of God can "divide soul from spirit" (Heb. 4:12). It presents the tension of vacillating between two concepts. On one hand there are the standards and ideologies of the world that we are born into with its emphasis on rationality, academia and science. On the other hand there is the factual nature of our existence with evidence of a subconscious or spiritual life external to our rational existence referencing the God of whom the Bible speaks. If we would listen, the Bible engages our minds, wills and emotions to recognize the incorporeal and our own spiritual existence. It purposes that the choice of life is to know God, through Jesus Christ. The cliffhanger experience challenges our logical existence and consequently, our relationship with God. The Word of God reveals that it is crucial to relinquish the demand of self will for God's will. On the cliff, individuals face major life-changing moments which cause them to waiver between these two demands. In the circumstances of the cliff hanger there is chaos requiring choice which has consequences on spiritual development. How a person responds during the cliffhanger experience effects spiritual maturation. The cliff hanger has positive or negative effects and is a valuable tool in the determination of an individual's spiritual knowledge and growth.

At first approach of the mountain, many are often taken aback by its massive size and height. You take a deep breath as you imagine scaling this majestic element; and then realize it is a mountain that you *must* scale. Its height has to be conquered and the first thing that comes to the natural mind is that you cannot do it. If aided by religious conviction, you may acknowledge that you are utterly incapable of the task in and of yourself and begin to seek assistance apart from the human self through the spiritual self. Even then the mountain taunts and menaces. It condemns at every onset of relief with regard to your capabilities. There is a constant reminder that you must change your perspective and your dependency on your wisdom to accomplish the feat that is set before you. Inch by inch you scale the mountain before you, only able to see the small area that you occupy. As you travel, you have become unaware of its significantly vertical formation. Once at the top, most have in mind that they have conquered this mountain by their own strategies, strength and commitment. Standing there atop the mountain, you encounter the cliff. A command on your life was the motivation for the journey and the crest of the mountain is where you are now standing. If this was the call of God, it has not been easy. It has been arduous getting here and now this cliff beckons you to relinquish reasoning and leap. It is hard to imagine that here at the cliff's edge the course of action is to jump. Its slopes make it impossible to simply climb down. The desire is to go back the way you came. Yet, you know this is not an option. The strategies, strengths and commitment that you utilized to conquer the mountain have no effect here at the top. You are exhausted from the climb and now from the stress of decision. To return to your old self, your old ways is not the advantage of being at the cliff. At this juncture, you realize that it is apparently time for a change in attitude, relationships and lifestyles. But, the human nature is often fearful of change; even when the eventual outcomes are beneficial. But do we really know the outcome? How can we be sure? What will happen? Thomas Carlyle *wrote: To reform a world, to reform a nation, no wise man will undertake; And all but foolish men know, that the only solid, though far slower reformation, is what each begins and perfects on himself.*[4] Sometimes the event at the cliff is private; just as every true Believer has an individual, personal encounter with God. Other times the event is public and the world is watching. Each episode has the goal of promoting God's plan of redemption. Each child of God has the stewardship of delivering the message of God by supplying an accurate portrayal of biblical teaching which is Agape—Christian love. While challenging ideologies, the cliffhanger encourages spiritual development. The Cliffhanger creates tension between the comfort, peace and sure conviction of faith based on the foundations of the Word of God and the laborious, speculative reasoning of men.

For those who believe, knowledge of grace is increased with the development and growth of one's spirituality toward Jesus as Lord. The grace of the gospel is an unmerited gift and described as someone having favor or chosen to be shown an act of kindness. The biblical record reveals that faith and grace are given by God (I Cor. 12:11; Eph. 4:7). Based on this premise, our spiritual maturation requires abandoning traditional ideas, removing expectation relative to performance and behaviors and accepting God's *imputed righteousness*. Paul says: "for what the law could not do, in that it was weak through the flesh, God sending His own Son in the likeness of sinful flesh, and for sin, condemned sin in the flesh; *the imputed righteousness means* that the righteousness of the law might be fulfilled in us, who walk not after the flesh, but after the Spirit" (Rom. 8:3-4; *emphasis*). For the Christian, accepting the *imputed righteousness* of God is our reciprocity of His grace. This is the reciprocity that empowers our responses at the cliff. Reciprocity is demonstrated as momentous movement toward God. Grace means we have been delivered and with the endowment of grace there is the manifestation of God presenting an indwelling desire to grow stronger in Him (II Tim. 1:9). Reciprocity of His grace reveals the principle: *to believe is to obey*. Proof that one is a child of God is obedience; according to James 2:20, "faith without *demonstrated* works of obedience is dead." Although grace is free and faith is given by measure, when our cliff experience reveals acceptances and obedience it encompasses the divinely apportioned act of human will and spirit. Jesus is our example, "He trusted no one, and never placed His faith in people yet, he was never suspicious or bitter. His confidence in God and what God's grace could do was so perfect that He never despaired and never gave up hope"[5] Grace elevates the created above the condition of his natural tendencies and reciprocity of this grace extends the reality of a new nature causing spiritual reflection to engender an elevated life. The cliff validates the inevitability of destruction and prompts subsequent submission to God's command. Grace is participation in the Divine, demonstrated as gratitude and allegiance; and spiritual development and maturity affirms the need of grace. Gratitude is an obligatory grateful heart expressing the sense of debt owed for God's sacrificial gift illustrated through Christ's obedience; and allegiance is exemplified as holy living, apart from human inadequacy, in preparation for a future reward. Human inadequacy finds its origin in a perverted will. Satan, a fallen cherub, who, although created perfectly with power, authority and a free will, became haughty upon perceiving his own splendor and sinned against God (Ezek. 28:12-19). Like Satan, man wants to exalt himself above God or *to be like God* (Gen. 3:5; Is. 14:13). According to the *Wycliffe Bible Commentary*, the heart of divinely created man was clean at the start, but having been given the power of choice and subjected to the power of "the tempter," the inevitable fall from grace happened because of mankind's desire to follow his own will.[6] Peter writes, that many will fall away from the faith once believed, by following false teachers and the "way of truth will be blasphemed. For if God did not spare angels when they sinned, but cast them into hell to be kept until judgment . . . *still* the Lord knows how to rescue the godly from trials and to keep the unrighteous under punishment . . . and especially those who indulge in the lust of defiling passion and despise authority" (II Pet. 2:1-4, 9, 10). Spiritual formation, through an allotment of grace can occur at the pinnacle of decision for Divinely created unbelievers and Believers alike. The juxtaposition of principles and perspectives reveal that, even Believers who have been forgiven their sins; who have been justified and made perfectly right with God, through the reckoning to them the righteousness of Jesus Christ, suffer the consequences of choices, often noted as a fall from grace.

As you contemplate Scriptures from the Word of God to assist and transport you along life's journey, like being "more than a conqueror" and able to "do all things through Christ," step by step layers of the natural man are removed, whether male or female, and the realization that this life's purpose is based upon an extraordinary premise outside of the self is revealed (Rom. 8:37; Phil.4:13). This extraordinary revelation of purpose may be portrayed in the natural realm by the history of nineteenth century female mountain climbers. The first women mountaineers contended with tremendous social, psychological and physical obstacles. However, each woman was indeed committed to overcoming these insurmountable odds with the final applause extended to the God of all mountains. According to *Women on High,* women tackled the mountains for recreation, adventure, challenge, escape or serenity despite the deterrents from narrow human perspectives.[7] They were women from diverse backgrounds, many of whom contended with being accompanied by lawless, destructive guides and males that were resistant to female leadership. Aside from the Bible, society dictates what constitutes normal female behaviors, so there were societal pressures regarding their aberrant behaviors and the allowable female attire conflicted with the required apparel for mountain climbing which further contributed to their struggles and frustrations. Many women wore undergarments which exerted as many pounds of pressure as their own weight on their midsections which, aside from bearing this additional extreme weight, caused difficulty breathing as they climbed harrowing slopes. These women were noted to have scaled mountains wearing long, flowing skirts, corsets and boots. Their clothing weighed roughly three times the weight of the technical clothing worn today and because they were women, these mountaineers were not afforded the proper and necessary equipment. Categorically rejecting the gender biases and societal limitations placed on women, they defied convention, set their sights toward an uncharted area, raised, tucked, pinned and sometimes hid their skirts; and refusing to be denied, stood upon some of the world's highest peaks. Their efforts were in opposition with the rational mind, especially regarding women in the early nineteenth century. The exhibition of humankind's life of struggles, frustrations, successes, failures, rivalries and greed is portrayed by the historicity of women mountaineers. Each woman demonstrated a purpose that challenged the intellect and each displayed an inner demand for triumph which was unveiled visibly. The choices made and the attainment of their purpose brought each woman to the awareness that the turmoil of absurdity wrought from society and within themselves when confronted and acknowledged, "strengthened the spirit, bringing a renewed courage and buoyancy."[8] Jesus equates the Christian to a man who builds his house knowing it will be tested in Matthew chapter 7 verses 24 and 25. Yet, regardless of questionable circumstances, obedience to God brings survival, protection and beneficial outcomes at the cliff. The cliffhanger provides narrative for experience, failure and accomplishment fashioned by the tension between faith and reason. With the proper perspective on God the natural mind and the spiritual heart are developed through testing.

Standing on the cliff there is a causal effect which means each action elicits a response which can be positive and negative. A struggle ensues between rational existence and supernatural promise. For the Christian, God is real and accessible through Jesus Christ. Jesus stated emphatically that "whoever has seen me has seen the Father," otherwise, to most people God is an invisible, impersonal or unimaginable being (John 14:9, ESV). The cliff hanger is a call to confirmation, commitment, conflict, change and the consequence of conviction. The presentation of these elements is crucial for redemption. This means that we should be conscious of each element with every cliff experience and recognize how each of them affects who we are and what we do. Each element impacts decision making and are fulfilled by the many choices imposed throughout life. Opportunity to establish commitment, experience consequence, externalize conflict, receive confirmation and reveal change is introduced during times on the cliff where faith and comprehension of grace are challenged. The acknowledgment of faith and the acceptance of grace are often celebrated prior to spiritual maturation. The cliffhanger is a transitory step in the journey of life that has the capacity to lead the Believer to transcend the mundane, being allowed to encounter the grace of a personal God and build on their relationship of faith. God states, in Scripture, that those who honor Him, He will honor (I Sam. 2:30). Sometimes reason attempts to stand in the way of faith. Many situations require simple obedience. God wants our trust.

In spite of popular opinion our faith and acceptance of God's grace through Jesus Christ does not lead to "happily ever after" in an earthly sense. Being born again ushers us into a marvelous relationship, spiritual condition and citizenship in the Kingdom of God. Still, the Bible informs us that our opposition is "against principalities, powers, rulers of darkness of this world and spiritual wickedness in high places" (Eph. 6:12). When faced with decision at the edge of the cliff we must be mindful of the subtlety of Satan who desires to destroy the plan of God. According to *Spiritual Depression*, the work of God, which Satan is most "anxious to destroy, is the work of grace in and through our Lord and Savior Jesus Christ."[9] This is a direct assault on faith and faith has a direct correlation to salvation. The Bible states in Hebrews chapter eleven verse six: "without faith it is impossible please God, for he who comes to God must believe that He is and that He is a rewarder of those who diligently seek Him." The reward is salvation. Salvation is deliverance from the fate of sin. The Bible says: "the wages of sin is death but the free gift of God is eternal life in Christ Jesus, our Lord" (Rom. 6:23). Each cliff's edge divulges our faith and the response on the cliff exhibits our faith. The *great cloud of witnesses* in Hebrews chapter eleven illustrates the necessity of cliff decisions to effect spiritual development and growth (Heb. 12:1). The *great clouds of witnesses are* people who have lived lives of faith, making the choice to follow God when confronted with decision at the cliff. Faith characterizes "fixing our eyes on Jesus, the author and perfecter of faith," which enables us to make manifest the will and purposes of God in our lives and for humanity (Heb. 12:2). Conversely, if the grace of God is met with confusion and denial of justification through faith alone, the result is an ineffectual doctrinal decision-making and inadequacy in the perceived will of God. The Israelites journey through the wilderness with Moses is an accounting of a people's lack of faith where millions died because of unbelief and separation from God never receiving God's reward. They proved that it is possible to establish oneself outwardly as children of God without ever actually being faithful to the Lord. For the unbeliever, it can be distinguished by the hardened heart and reluctance to accept that which is deemed unreasonable. Hebrews 3:8-9 affirms that even when individuals witness the miraculous and observe victory over various episodic predicaments, many choose to sit in judgment of God, despite having had incredible encounters with Him and the awesome demonstration of His power (Num. 14:11). Grace suggests that we must choose to respond to God's voice. The Book of Numbers, discloses a people who, as a nation historically, did not discern or respond to the will of God. During their time on the cliff, while at the edge of the wilderness, they exhibited disobedience and an absence of faith. There is the account of the twelve spies who ignored the declaration of God regarding the Promised Land. Naturally, it did not make sense to go into a land where men of exceptional strength and giants were the adversary. Joshua and Caleb remained steadfast in their belief of the Lord's promise, demonstrating that spiritual maturity is guided by persevering faith (Num. 14:9; 32:12). Trusting in the knowledge and will of God, rejoicing in salvation and patiently enduring even through suffering, as a testament to the grace of God, one's faith perseveres. The Word of God says to make sure of your calling (I Pet. 5:10). "How long will you waiver between two opinions?"(I Kings 18:21) Our spiritual growth journey is a process of spiritual development by faith. It is the expression of a deeper, powerful relationship in God and others. The spiritual work afforded by grace takes time, effort, patience, commitment and faith. A life of faith entails action. "By faith Abel offered, Noah prepared, Abraham obeyed, Moses chose and Rahab welcomed" (Heb. 11:4, 7, 8, 24-25, 31). The cliffhanger reminds Christians that the gospel message involves the whole man; "love the Lord your God with all your heart and with all your soul and with all your strength and with all your mind" (Luke 10:27). It exhorts that the Christian should hold onto hope, being "able to give reason for the hope that is in Him" (I Pet.3:15):

> The child of God has received the message of Jesus and the resurrection as truth. He is enlightened by the Holy Spirit and having seen the truth, his heart is moved and he loves it. Now seeing what he was; the life he has lived, he hates it when he sees the glorious truth about the love of God. Now, you want it, are moved by it and cannot help that your greatest desire is to live it.[10]

A cliffhanger is often the ending to a story, or an ending which leaves the story unfinished. It is a literary device in fictional narratives which features a main character in a precarious situation, a difficult dilemma, confronting a shocking revelation or seemingly impossible circumstances. The idea of the cliffhanger is that the main character of the story has reached the pinnacle of their mountain. In a fictional story, the audience is prompted to return to see how the dilemma is resolved; in real life, being left at the edge of a cliff is not so sensationalized. There are many mountains and many cliffs in this life. The mountain teaches a lot of things. It teaches how ambiguous the world of people is, and their cares; how we place so much faith in the insecurity of the world and how questionable life is outside of knowing God, through Jesus Christ. This should be the reality, since Jesus affords acceptance by God and accessibility to Him. The character of Jesus ought to be reproduced in the Believer as the fruit of the Spirit, demonstrated by love for God and love for His people (Mat. 22: 37-40). The essence of the cliffhanger experience is that it necessitates choice during the disruptive events of life to effect relationship with God and every choice influences spiritual maturity.

For our gospel did not come to you in word only, but also in power and in the Holy Spirit and with full conviction.

I Thess. 1:5

CHAPTER TWO

A Call to Confirmation

Confirmation has many synonyms. It can mean authorization, affirmation, evidence, authentication, proof, substantiation and corroboration. Confirmation indicates the child of God has the requisite responsibility to provide verifiable proof of faith. The Word of God emphasizes that confirmation is faith, practice, theology, life, doctrine and conduct. James wrote: "show me your faith without the works, and I will show you my faith by my works; *and* for just as the body without the spirit is dead, so also faith without works is dead." (James 2:18, 26). Jesus' own examples include: "Let your light so shine before men, that they may see your good works and glorify your Father in heaven *and* whoever denies Me before men, him I will also deny before My Father who is in heaven" (Mat. 5:16; 10:33). Faith is not static. There must be progression and development even in its practice. As a call to confirmation, Children of the Most High God have the authorization to introduce others to the Father. The Bible states that the Believer "must be born again" to receive this authorization. To be born again establishes the Christian as a re-created spirit in Christ and that Jesus' heritage belongs to those persons who are now reborn by the Holy Spirit (John 3:3; Gal. 2:20; 4:6-7). The Word of God has extended a formal notice of empowerment to every Believer. Consequently, each individual Believer is given the right to discipleship and priesthood with the commission to teach the gospel and disciple-making (I Pet. 2: 5, 9;

Mat. 28: 19-20). Believers have the affirmation as spiritual heirs of the Truth. "The Holy Spirit, Himself testifies with our spirit that we are children of God, and if children, heirs also, heirs of God and fellow heirs with Christ; therefore you belong to Christ as heirs according to promise" (Rom. 8:16-17; Gal. 3:29). Faith is exhibited as the proof of this truth. Faith is demonstrated as a supernatural belief that is transcendent to natural tendency. A call to confirmation means substantiation through Jesus Christ. Even unbelievers have heard historical accounts of Jesus' existence. The Bible provides exposition on His life's work, crucifixion and resurrection. A call to confirmation becomes the indisputable acceptance of the knowledge and reality of Jesus Christ. It is evidenced by an effectual and radical transformation of the heart and mind resulting in the spiritual growth and development of a spirit-imbued humanity. Confirmation means authentication by exemplifying Jesus. Following His ascension, the Holy Spirit came to set apart the genuine heirs of salvation. By grace, receipt of the Holy Spirit through choice is the seal of this relationship and guarantees a life modeled after Jesus. "The fruit of God's Spirit: love, joy, peace, patience, kindness, goodness, faithfulness, gentleness, and self-control" is the means of identifying individuals and verifying their eligibility as children of God (Gal. 5:22-23). In the bond of unity it becomes necessary to demonstrate corroboration as a community of Believers "showing forth God's praise" (Ps.106: 2). The insistence in God's Word is that we must put away anger and wrath, learn to do the good we can for all; and put on compassion and kindness, ceasing to do evil:

> As those who have been chosen of God, holy and beloved; put on a heart of compassion, kindness, humility, gentleness and patience; bearing with one another, and forgiving each other. Whoever has a complaint against anyone; just as the Lord forgave you, so also should you *forgive others*. Beyond all these things *put on* love, which is the perfect bond of unity. Let the peace of Christ rule in your hearts, to which indeed you were called in one body; and be thankful (Col. 3:12-15).

For the Christian, life is a miracle and life in Christ is a sacred gift from God. The Bible is the Holy writ, a formal written order, and provides the Christian with principles for living which is to love God first over and above anything else and secondly, to love others unconditionally (Mat. 19:19; Luke 10:30-37). The Word of God proclaims: "God has shown you, O man, what is good; and what does the LORD require of you but to do justly, to love mercy, and to walk humbly with your God?"(Micah 6:8) Therefore, a confirmed Christian is embodied by a life purposed for God. Confirmation is observed as a state of reverence and thanksgiving to God and the Believer has a compulsion to care for others (I John 5:3). Love for God is the motivation and is apparent through obedience to His commands. Love for God transforms thinking, disposition and habits. Acts of service, charitable giving of time, talent and treasure; concerns for justice and truth are displayed in life as the Believer affirms that hope is in the realm of the spiritual. In stark contrast to a life unconfirmed in Christ, the child of God behaves like they owe their life to God. As the bible states: "anyone in Christ, *is* a new creation; old things have passed away; behold, all things have become new" (II Cor. 5:17). Confirmation is developed through cliff experiences which achieves affirmatively observable indications of a change in spiritual perspective.

During the initiation of the Kingdom of God, our Lord warned his disciples to prepare for persecution. To sustain on the journey and to substantiate Christianity, they were to avoid all things which gave advantage to the enemies of Christ: all meddling with worldly or political concerns which are conspicuously self-seeking and divisive (although government and God are distinct, they were not to be in opposition), all appearance of evil or selfishness, and all unscrupulous and clandestine dealings (Mat. 22:15-22; John 19: 8-15; Eph. 4:14-27). Christ foretold troubles, not only that the troubles might not be a surprise, but that they might confirm their faith. It would be beyond glorious to live free from the burdens of living in this world, but as children of God this is not the case. The cliffhanger divulges a life that is often counter to the mundane practices and attitudes. One finds that the general events of life and its circumstances instigate irritations and confusion in individuals determined to follow God's way. The call to confirmation presumes that if we truly trust and believe God's redemptive plan, contend for the faith, live the character of Jesus as obedient servants to God and His Word we receive His peace. God's peace is unaffected by the world; although those who have faith in redemption and restoration through Jesus Christ will not always find that their choices are easy. It appears clearly in the Bible, that all who live a confirmed life in Christ Jesus must suffer persecution, tribulation and trials (Mat. 5:10-12; Mark 4:17; Acts 14:22; James 1:2). Persecutors are tormentors, bullies or oppressors who prey upon the meek or have hardened hearts lacking comprehension of spiritual things and of the impartiality of grace. Relationships, bonds of love and duty have been irreparably broken by persecutors from enmity against Christ. Jesus said, "A prophet is not without honor except in his own country, among his own relatives, and in his own house" (Mark 6:4). Therefore, followers of Jesus must expect to enter into the kingdom of God through many tribulations and much testing while having an observable level of intimacy in their relationship with the Father and Son as an affirmation of faith (2 Pet. 3:12). The restored relationship in Jesus and the faith that secures it are the cause of joy and peace, even in the midst of uncertainty (Phil. 4:7). This relationship is based upon the Believer having seen the cross which reveals the love of God, the Father, Jesus, the Son and His Holy Spirit. The cliff tests and deepens faith. Although an outcry may be expressed in the reality of what is happening; there is faith in its outcome.

When Jesus sent His disciples on assignment they were instructed to go without funds, food, extra clothing and gear. He was teaching them to trust God for provisions 'for the laborer is worthy of his wages" (Luke 10:1-7). Later the disciples were instructed to take what was needed for the journey, indicating that they had already received provision from God. God is the provider of all provisions; for everything is His. The Bible confirms that "without faith it is impossible to please Him who is a rewarder of those who believe that He *exists and is God*; and diligently seek Him" (Heb. 11:6, *emphasis*). Inevitably, the disciples had to proceed with His teachings and the substantiation through miracles of the Lord without His physical presence. Although experiencing moments on the cliff was not new to them, this initial time on the edge without visibly seeing Jesus had to be an uncomfortable place. Can God really be trusted to take care of us? Should we no longer always plan ahead? Besides, if we "go" as He has instructed, where will we stay? Where are we going?

Who is this other Comforter? Do we abandon all senses? How can we? Walking in genuine faith evidenced by total surrender is required of every disciple. God has designed His Kingship to be confirmed as divine rule among humankind (Mat. 4:17-25). How do we make known God's call on our lives? It is by living our faith with actions and words as proof unto God. Many times the cliff is experienced as a disruption of life's routine, individual priorities and often peace of mind. It can depress economic and social claims, redirect loyalties and create new relationships. The cliffhanger challenges perceived normalcy. Response to this challenge prompts recognition of the Believer's position in Jesus Christ. When viewed as God's agenda, it allows the Believer to participate in God's purposes. Each occurrence of struggle and trial, crisis of faith, intimacy with death and lies we believe discloses options that offer opportunity to discern His perspectives relative to particular situations and as a result yields opportunity for spiritual maturity. The pinnacle of decision is a call to confirmation for unbelievers, also. There upon the mountain peak is a time to evaluate the evidence, corroborate the proofs, authenticate and acquire authorization; and affirm truths. The natural inference is that unbelievers do not recognize the spirituality of their circumstances. They thrive on the belief that situations are meted out as fate, and the results of success or failure as the product of actions. In the midst of trials, tribulations and suffering certainly their heart is broken and their conscience is smitten. What defense do they have? Sometimes in the solitary recesses of the mind, even the unbeliever's spirit is acknowledged, spiritual enlightenment occurs and acceptance is established.

Struggles and Trials to Overcome

> *Let the wise hear and increase in learning, and the one who understands obtain guidance, to understand a proverb and a saying, the words of the wise and their riddles.*
>
> Proverbs 1:5, 6

Confirmation may be described as the act of affirming the truth. The accuracy or genuineness of one's belief is often evidenced through struggles, trials, temptations, sorrows and crises. What does struggles, trials, temptations, sorrows and crises have to do with confirmation? Many people wrestle with considerable burden. Some quietly, alone or with close family and friend; others publicly, garnering media attention. But, regardless how it is experienced, there is a necessary awareness of powerlessness which entails confrontation of one's spirituality. Coming to terms with life with its many fractured moments and many opportunities of despair is truly a test of fortitude. Life's temptations and trials are struggles which test an individual's mettle, the Believer's faith in Christ, and obedience to God's Word. Even for persons who doubt the existence of God or the Truths of the Bible, struggles and trials lead to making choices based on the spiritual realm where good and evil reign. It is essential to recognize our weakness; how little control we have in any situation and take responsibility for our choices to prevail over trials and temptations. Sometimes we place blame on others for the choices we make. Sometimes we blame ourselves, when oftentimes our circumstances may be limited by the choices of others. Some have a tendency to rationalize their behavior or to make excuses. When we misplace blame for our choices or circumstances, God can never change us. He desires our confirmation as demonstrated by His generous gift of life through Christ. Christ's earthly struggles, trials, temptations, sorrows and crises were for expiation and propitiation. Expiation emphasizes the removal of guilt through a payment of the penalty (redemption), while propitiation emphasizes the appeasement or averting of God's wrath and justice (atonement). Both words are associated with our reconciliation. Christ's death on the cross for our sins has reconciled us to God (Romans 5:9-11; 2 Corinthians 5:18-21; Colossians 1:19-23). God offers His Word and Holy Spirit for our strengthening, sustaining and sanctifying. In spite of the many struggles and trials in this world, the Believer has been endowed with the image of the Creator (Gen. 1:27). Following receipt of His Holy Spirit, Christians are guided to be triumphant and not accept the simple humanity that commands us. We are much more than the physical man which dies daily; our life entails much more than this natural life and our future shines much brighter far longer than we can imagine. Often standing over the chasm at the cliff's edge is the time to gain the knowledge that, in the midst of struggles, trials, temptations and sorrows, people of God are set apart and are to live a confirmed life, proven, strengthened, and sanctified in Him. We must affirm this Truth by our confirmation to choose what God has to offer.

Life is full of troubles and in them we can become humble and learn that we are not alone. Our predicaments will not make us humble; our attitude toward them will. To be humble is defined as exercising the qualities of being modest, patient and teachable. Being humble requires an ability to hold back negative emotion. Sometimes our Lord decides to chasten His people by trying their patience and faith; testing their knowledge of Him and relationship with Him. In our trials, temptations, sorrows and struggles we must humble ourselves, which means understanding and accepting our limitations, recognizing our faults, acknowledging our mistakes, not comparing ourselves to others, deferring any judgment and realizing who has the power for transformation. If we choose not to be humble, this will only draw us further away from our Savior. There may be times when people feel that temptations or trials would be easier, and struggles and sorrows lessened if the Lord would bless with miracles, signs and wonders. In these circumstances, desperately seeking a solution, without much forethought you fling yourself over the mountain anticipating that everything will be taken care of by your Heavenly Father who you know as the one who narrates the beginning and the end. The message of the Word of God which is alive, powerful and sharper than any double-edged sword is that *no one should tempt God* (Mat.4:7). But when God is chosen unequivocally, without expectation or recourse, through just believing by faith, the Holy Spirit can manage the mind, will and emotions to produce a humble spirit and deliver the evidence in and through circumstances, of the Believer's confirmation in the Lord (II Cor. 2:14; I Thess. 2).

You are employed at a major corporation that, even in a recession, has seen tremendous growth. You receive a request to attend a meeting to discuss the future of the company. Once there you are informed that due to severe market fluctuations it has become necessary to adjust the budget and this requires workforce reduction. As the department manager you have been asked to compile a list of employees who could be considered unessential. It is a grueling task because you have to identify people you know and trust, people who trust you and individuals that you know have gone the extra mile for the company. Much to your chagrin, you are being asked to compile a list of friends, long-standing coworkers and newcomers to the organization with new homes, new families and future dreams. When you present the list to your administrator you are told that, regrettably, you must write your name at the bottom of the list. You do not know what to think. You have devoted 15, 20, 25, or as many as thirty years of service to this company. What does this say about the value of your work or about the integrity of the leadership? What does it mean for your future? How will this affect your family and since you are nearing the age to retire where will you go from here? Your mountain journey has led you to the cliff. It is the kind of moment when all that has been before, all that is now and all that is to come suddenly needs to be reinterpreted and you feel that you need an interpreter. Human experience includes individual and collective struggles and triumphs which are played out in the spirit of mankind as well as in the natural or physical realm. These experiences have identity, environment and internal landscape which often expose social constructs and roles beyond our control. The cliff's edge exhibits our capability to find balance between our limitations and a limitless God.

In the Book of Genesis, Jacob was given an assignment. God was leading him in a new direction with a new perspective saying "I am the God *of* Bethel, where you anointed a pillar, where you made a vow to Me; now arise, leave this land, and return to the land of your birth; I will surely prosper you and make your descendants as the sand of the sea, which is too great to be numbered" (Gen. 31:13; 32:12). But, before proceeding, it was known that Jacob would resist due to his unbelief so, there had to be a fight. He had to wrestle with God and men, and make amends with his brother Esau prior to returning to his homeland to satisfy His charge in God's purpose (Gen. 32: 28). Jacob, one of the many descendants of Abraham was the second born twin of Isaac and Rebekah. The firstborn was named Esau. Both are representative of the best and the worst of human nature, demonstrating the moral, physical, social and intellectual struggles and trials that encompass humanity and our ongoing need for a savior. Both sons had a future inheritance to *father a nation* and both had special mountain paths to follow which led to a struggle between the two of them. From the beginning, in their mother's womb, they "jostled each other" (Gen. 27:22). Jacob, whose name figuratively means *deceives*, grasped the heel of his brother at childbirth, even then, seemingly zealous for power. After they grew into manhood, Esau sold his birthright as the firstborn to Jacob and Jacob deceived his father Isaac, into giving him the blessing meant for the firstborn. To escape an enraged brother, Jacob was subject to a long period of exile from his relatives and the comfort of familiar surroundings. He journeyed to the land of his mother's birth at her recommendation to find a suitable mate. There Jacob acquired much wealth and a large family of his own through deceit and cunning. However, Jacob's experience on the metaphorical mountain introduced his transformation into a man fit for God's purpose. During his initial encounter with God, God promised to return Jacob to his homeland. A contract was established as reaffirmation of the Abrahamic Covenant and to confirm the reality of God for Jacob (Gen. 28:14). This reality was initially met with ambivalence (Gen. 28:20-21). When he learned of his brother Esau's presence in the land of his exile with a large group of men, Jacob faced his time of decision at the edge of the mountain. Did this mean that his brother was still angry? Has he come for revenge? How could Jacob protect his family? What can be done to prevent what seemed an inescapable encounter? What can he barter for his safety? Did not God promise to return Jacob to his homeland? Where is God now? Jacob sent a series of gifts in an attempt to appease his brother. Struggle had always been predominant with Jacob and Jacob struggled with faith as his maneuvers signify. While preparing for the inevitable meeting with his brother, in the dark of night a man of God wrestled with Jacob at the cliff's edge. Faith versus unbelief was the contest. So unlike his grandfather, Abraham, who humbly and powerfully served God or his father, Isaac, who passively submitted to God; Jacob who was crafty and self-centered chose negotiation and bargaining for God's favor. Grappling with mankind's natural inclination of doubt and sovereignty, at the climax of the contest, Jacob realized that he had seen the Lord and inconceivably, he lived (Gen. 32: 30). He wrestled with God and man. God won and Jacob gave his life over to Him but not without a permanent reminder of his defiance (Gen. 32: 24, 31-32). After that night Jacob died to self-confidence, admitted his insolence and confessed that he was a deceiver. Following this encounter, God changed his name to Israel (Gen. 32:28). Although

Jacob lost the altercation in the physical, he won a major spiritual victory. His time on the cliff ushered in a transformation which had a significant impact on his spiritual maturity. As evidence of his conversion, he erected an altar and called it El-Elohe-Israel; God, the God of Israel" (Gen. 33:20). Day after day individuals reach a point on the mountain when they long for spiritual truth. Struggles, temptations and trials stimulate the need to seek God and know His ways. Many come demanding; eager for God to come near to assist them rather than beseeching the security of a relationship with Him "as if they were a nation that does what is right and has not forsaken the commands of God" (Is. 58:2-14). The cliffhanger allows a person to be distinctly changed through struggles and trials by the reality and love of God; and confirmed through the guidance of His Holy Spirit. The victory belongs to God.

The Intimacy of Death

Help my unbelief. Mark 9:24

Intimacy with death provokes reason. Reason strives for the expression of truth. According to Oswald Chambers the eternal soul of mankind is expressed rationally by the spirit and whenever the Holy Spirit empowers the soul it does not contradict it but rationally transcends it.[11] At the edge of your cliff you must decide whether to make reason the center of life or God. According to Second Corinthians chapter 10, verse 5, thoughts, ideas, reasoning and philosophies are the barriers used by individuals against God and the message of the Gospel. Therefore, the intimacy of death necessitates a leap of faith that literally takes one's breath away as it defies human reason. The Bible indicates that faith is the catalyst for miracles. The leper was cleansed, the Centurion servant was healed and demons were cast into swine all due to the faith of the individual requesting the miracle. In Mark chapter Nine, a boy possessed by a demon which induced the inability to speak, caused dangerously violent body convulsions and required constant supervision for his protection, had a father that, although he believed the observed capabilities and eyewitness reports about Jesus; his reason said that the feat to cast out the demons that were in his son would be impossible. Faith is necessary to discipline reason. The father said to Jesus, "Do something if you can" (Mark: 9:22). "What do you mean, if I can? Jesus asked. Anything is possible *if a person believes*, the father instantly replied: I do believe but, help my *lack of faith*" (Mark 9: 22-24, NLT, *emphasis*). He believed that God could do the impossible, but was disheartened by reason's pervasive irrationality. Faith is a spiritual manifestation and the means by which the things of God are accomplished. Reason is a part of the intellectual, natural world that, without the supernatural power of God, is unable to comprehend faith and frustrates Divine connections. The father needed a faith that conquers doubt for healing to be achieved. At the mountain crest, overcome by fear, doubt and guilt, agonizingly the father entreated Jesus for relief. He labeled his disheartened station *unbelief.* Unbelief is described as fretful worrying, distrust, incredulity, apprehension and skepticism. Reason searches for concrete philosophies. The dad wanted release for his son from Satan who was working to destroy him. He wanted his son to live. The father's own spirit is seen as wilting under the strength of his rational mind while the spirit of God allowed him to stand strong in his faith. Faith empowers the human spirit and quiets reason, allowing spiritual maturity to develop on the edge of the cliff.

There comes a time in the life of every mortal to die; to leave these earthly vessels and earthly treasures are discarded. We are aware that this is the journey of everyone and no matter if the event is sudden, tragic, anticipated or predictable the emotions of loss prevail. When directed along the mountain path of impending death, insecurities, failures and frailties accompany us and we long for strength without suffering. More often the journey can become surreal as if the Heavenly Father protects us by insulating the mind. The cliff, or its characteristic of having no road ahead, is disguised to the reasoning mind yet provokes uncertainty; and with its uncertainty causes one to pause and often to implore the Creator for mercy. It has been reported that even the unbelieving will cry out for mercy mindful that mercy can come from *somewhere*. It appears that after all of the machinations of mankind the proclivity of humanity is to strain for belief in God's miraculous power. Standing there peering into the darkness you still hold on to the hope that God can make things right, can't he? If the miracle depends on me, Lord, help me to keep believing; "increase *my* faith" (Luke 17:5). As reason searches the heart to offer support and apprehension, the heart cries *help my unbelief.* Seeing impending death progress to immediate, the souls of the one in need of care and the care giver blend together as each accepts their role and responsibility. Each has concern for the other and each is watchful of the other's presence and needs. Where do we go from here? How can we say good-bye without hurt? I am really going to miss them, why do they have to go? Why now? You realize, standing at the cliff's edge that it is not dark. God's Holy Spirit transcends circumstance, you become aware that God is with you and His angels encamp around you for protection. The Bible reminds us that "he who dwells in the secret place of the Most High, will abide under the shadow of the Almighty" (Ps. 91:1). The secret place is our experience of intimacy with Him and we are comforted. Stepping off the cliff is clearly the only direction from this mountain. Gently, there is an assurance regarding the matters at this cliff that surpasses human comprehension. "Christ will, even now as always, be exalted; whether by life or by death" (Phil. 1:20). At once, you come to a complete knowledge of God and the power of His resurrection. Amazingly, both of you are transitioned unto God, having been nurtured, demonstrably advanced spiritually and are now able to truly say, "O death, where is thy sting? O grave, where is thy victory?" (I Cor. 15:55). Illness can be physically, emotionally and psychologically painful to the sufferer. For some, there is a social stigma attached to it which only serves to alienate the person from family and friends. The cliff teaches that although we cannot always be sure of God's will, we can be sure of His wisdom and mercy. Confronted by the intimacy of death, at the pinnacle of the mountain we discover that those afflictions are blessed which bring us "to know Christ and Him crucified" which can cause us to seek His help and salvation (I Cor. 2:2). The shed blood of Christ has forgiven any guilt and His mercy frustrates any doubt. The call to confirmation at this juncture in life is in the attempt to move fearlessly, firmly, even if quietly in faith through the chaos. Standing face to face with mortality is complex. It can be defined as the ultimate cliffhanger experience. The prophet Isaiah admonishes God's people to hear the message of our Lord and be comforted for "He gives strength to the weary" and those who "lacks might He increases power" (Is. 40:1, 29). Death, disease and disability are constant reminders that the payment for sin of the natural life as we know it is permanent. But the Word of God tells us that what looks to men like defeat is victory in the eyes of God (Col. 2:15).

The narrative of John the Baptist presents one who prepared the way for Jesus' coming and called the Jewish people to repentance. He is identified with the Prophet Elijah, as he spoke out boldly; speaking God's words of warning to a people who sometimes drifted from their teachings. But Jesus gave the acknowledgment that there had been "no one born of women greater than John" (Mat. 11:11). John, God's messenger, was born to Elizabeth, the relative of Jesus' mother, Mary. Filled with the Holy Spirit from birth, he lived an ascetic life and was noted as "one crying in the wilderness," preaching and baptizing in preparation for the coming Kingdom of God (Luke 1:15, 57-80). He spoke to the masses inciting expectation and preparation for the coming Messiah. He rebuked the Scribes and Pharisees saying: "O generation of vipers, who has warned you to flee from the wrath to come?" (Luke 3:7). He exhorted all to repent of their sins and prepare for the coming Day of Judgment. He demonstrated an active faith as he preached about the ensuing Kingdom of God to be established through Jesus and urged many to repent and be baptized saying: "He who is coming after me is mightier than I, and I am not fit to remove His sandals; He will baptize you with the Holy Spirit and fire"(Mat.3:11). When Jesus arrived to find John baptizing, Jesus received this baptism and John introduced Him to the public as the "Christ." John confronted the sins of the community no matter who was involved. He spoke out against the sins of the Israel ruler, King Herod Antipas. John boldly preached against Herod's adulterous marriage to his brother's wife, Herodias. He knew that his words were antagonistic and to continue asserting this issue could likely lead to his death. It is written that John's voice was commanding and therefore hard to ignore. He was ordained to speak forward the truth of God's Word no matter the cost. With every word of reprimand he calculated the cost and there atop his mountain he became intimate with his own death. King Herod ordered John imprisoned so that he could no longer continue his attacks on Herod's marriage. Although he was removed from further influence, Herod's wife held a grudge against John for his reproach and wanted him put to death. But Herod protected John because he enjoyed listening to him regarding the coming new Kingdom and because the citizens of his kingdom revered John the Baptist as a prophet. Because of this some of John's disciples were allowed to visit him in prison and kept him informed of the works of Jesus. John the Baptist locked in prison and in danger of being executed found himself at the edge of the mountain with no land in sight. He was confronted by *unbelief.* He needed reassurance to affirm his faith. Has the promise of God truly been fulfilled during his lifetime? Is Jesus really the Messiah? His decision was to send word to Jesus, asking "are you the one who was to come, or should we expect someone else" (Luke 7:20)? He received his enlightenment and comfort from the Lord (Luke 7:22). John received the blessing of intimacy in Jesus Christ (Luke 7:23). When King Herod celebrated his birthday by hosting a banquet, during the feast, the daughter of Herodias danced before he and his guests. Her entertainment pleased King Herod and he swore to give her anything she requested, up to half of his kingdom. The young woman went to her mother for suggestions of what she should request. Herodias told her to ask for the head of John the Baptist. The daughter asked for his head on a platter. King Herod was remorseful upon hearing this request, but because of his oath, and the favored reputation of his dinner guests, Herod ordered the beheading of John. John's experience on the precipice refined his spiritual growth, receiving confirmation of Jesus the Messiah, had to impart quietness and confidence as his strength. The grandeur and majesty of the mountain is often taken for granted. During the crisis of illness and the intimacy of death for all concerned the experience on the cliff requires a Spirit induced sane decision through meditation and reflection which can lead to a new appreciation of life, prayer, relationships, and opportunities for service. It can have a profound effect on spiritual development. The crisis of faith which will be discussed later is often conquered through intimacy with death.

Sorrowful, Yet Always Rejoicing

For when I am weak, then I am strong.

II Corinthians 12:10

The Christian journey is filled with paradoxes: Faith encounters doubt, Truth wrestles with error, Good battles evil, strength is gained through weakness, light shines in darkness, gain through loss, joy through sorrow, life through death, and to live we must die. This is the atmosphere in which Christians exist. A paradox refers to opinions or ideas which are contrary. The concepts oppose each other, leading one to believe that they are totally contradictory when actually they indicate complimentary perspectives. To say that something is a paradox expresses that opposite viewpoints can both be right. The concept of law and grace for example; Jesus affirms fulfillment of the law by grace not by its abolishment. This is perceived as a conflict by many. Unfortunately, some cliffhanger experiences are based on false assumptions which cause conflict. In these instances if one side is certain of being right, any contrary idea must be wrong. As the individual seeks remedy for the tension that is faced while standing at the edge of the cliff, the need is for real and legitimate understanding. We must seek God for the wisdom to see the values of the trial to maintain a positive mental attitude and if we ask in faith without doubting we will receive the wisdom we need to obtain clarity as we endeavor to make our choice (James 1:2-5). Mankind does not have the ability to evaluate appropriately the value of our cliff experiences. What we discern as negative may actually have positive worth. Although we may never see the value of a trial, fear, ignorance, doubt and double-mindedness often causes us to miss the best of God. It requires faith to see the value of the cliff and although we try and believe we surmise its worth, one cannot know its value while experiencing it. "Blessed is the man who endures trials for when he has stood the test he will receive the crown of life which God has promised to those who love Him" (James 1:12). The Apostle Paul said that he felt "as chastened, and not killed; as sorrowful, yet always rejoicing; as poor, yet making many rich; as having nothing, yet possessing all things" (II Corinthians 6:9-10, KJV).

To many people a relationship between a holy God and sinful humanity is a paradox. It may sound contradictory though both complement each other through Jesus Christ; the fulfillment of law and grace. To the mundane world without faith in Christ, every belief in God has been publicized as parts of a greater whole distinguished by a perspective much like the story of the blind men who each touched individual, separate and distinct parts of an elephant. Each held different points of view as they were categorizing based on specific information. Each believed they were right in their judgment. Each blind man could argue without end and never convince the others to change their viewpoint. The issue could only be resolved by exchanging positions around the elephant to examine it from the others point of reference. Once everyone has the opportunity to consider all of the evidence then the probability of truth emerges. Paradox means that opposing perspectives can both be right. However, Jesus negates a paradoxical point of view when it pertains to God, as all people are sinners and in need of a savior. He announces that the only way to be saved is by Him (John 14: 16). It is natural for humans to hang on to a paradoxical idea because the Bible affirms that mankind follows their "father, Satan and want to carry out *his* desires" (John 8:44). When there are opposing views, each considered real and legitimate, it promotes disunity; and it becomes impossible for everyone to join the same side. However, the spiritual man, when religiosity and the philosophies of this natural world are discarded, is conscious of only one truth and the reality of only one side; dispelling the paradox. Mountain peaks, like high places, are slippery. The Word of God states that "the nail that is now fastened in the sure place shall be removed, and cut down, and fall (Is. 22: 25, KJV). Life's journey offers many twists and turns, ups and downs, even ins and outs along the way. The individual is mistaken who thinks that any place in this world is a sure place, or themselves as *nails fastened securely*; for there is nothing on this earth that is certain but uncertainty. Imagine that you are living your life to its fullest. You have a job or career that offers much satisfaction, family, friends, loved ones, opportunities for travel and your financial needs are met. God is really blessing you and your relationship with Him gives you peace. You have your life planned; you know where you are going and what you will do when you get there. Suddenly, unexpectedly, one day you receive news of astronomical proportions. You are devastated by the message of your demise. Your journey is soon over. Looking over the edge of the cliff you say to yourself, this can't be. I'm too young. How can this be when I have always been mindful to do the right thing? Because of your faith, you pray asking the *Lord to please remove this cup that I might not have to drink of it.* Realizing that there is no going back on this journey, as you jump off the cliff, faith is expressed: "Lord, not my will but yours be done" in and through my life (Luke 42:22). This is the choice for everyone. Once this choice is made, you start allowing the Lord freedom to orchestrate your life and align it according to His will with an observable joy and a fervor that the people around you cannot mistake. You begin taking on challenges directly related to the purposes of God in His Word, living each day one day at a time, finding solace through anguish, peace in perplexity and calm inside confusion. Just as Paul was given a thorn in the flesh, it does not matter whether or not you receive the promotion or degree you are seeking, are faced with divorce, illness or death; your choice to establish a relationship with God will sustain you, giving you a renewed strength, revealed purpose and a recognizable praise as your life has become a privilege in Him. People will not understand your pleasure in pain. But by putting off your old self, that was being corrupt by deceitful desires, which belongs to a former manner of life and the renewal of the mind by the Spirit, you aspire daily to true righteousness and holiness (Eph. 4:22-24). Those standing at the cliff's edge facing unexpected trials without faith in God are often "darkened in their understanding" (Eph. 4.12). However, faith is having a relationship with God that is revealed as hope and belief in the unseen where comprehension is exposed to the light of the Word and faith becomes manifest causing a transformation of how circumstances are processed. "Anything exposed by the Light becomes visible and anything that becomes visible is light" (Eph. 4.13-14). Once the truth is exposed, it becomes necessary to "discern what is pleasing to the Lord" aiding your resolve to choose the path which leads to eventual spiritual growth (Eph.4.10).

Before he was an apostolic leader of Christians, Saul of Tarsus was the leading nemesis of Christianity. He was the most notorious threat to the dissemination of the Gospel because he hated Christians. Born in the first century, the man known today as the Apostle Paul was born Saul to allegedly wealthy parents who were Diaspora Jews and migrated from Palestine to Tarsus, a city in what is now the country of Turkey. Tarsus was a Roman city, so Saul was born a Roman citizen which afforded a status that rendered many privileges. Saul was privy to Greek learning, philosophy, rhetoric, and athletics. He studied the Jewish religion, learned Hebrew and Aramaic. Therefore, he would have been quite educated; and both multilingual and multicultural. Studying under the well-respected Gamaliel, Saul mastered the Torah and the entire Jewish law, rising to the standing of a Pharisee (Acts 2:3). Saul (Paul) describes himself in his letters, as "blameless" in his conformity to Jewish law and "exceedingly zealous" in adherence to the Jewish religion (Phil. 3:6; Gal. 1:14). After the ascension of Jesus a new sect of Jews called "Christians" became relevant in Jerusalem spreading throughout the Roman world and beyond. These Christians proclaimed that Jesus of Nazareth had come as the Messiah, had been crucified, then rose from the dead; validating Jesus' messianic claims. Saul was in Jerusalem while the new Christian religion was proliferating and infuriated by rumors of Jesus' resurrection, he sided with those Jews who regarded Christian teachings as blasphemy. According to the book of Acts, Gamaliel was a moderate in his perspective toward Christians (Acts 5:34-38). This was not so with Saul, who aggressively persecuted Christians and was responsible for many of their deaths. One day Saul encountered Jesus on his way to Damascus (Acts 9). Although none of the others with him could see Jesus, Saul was blinded by this meeting. This encounter, as it does with everyone who has one, changed his life's direction and placed him on the crest of the mountain. Did he really see Jesus? Was not Jesus crucified? Had Yahweh sent this Jesus to rebuke him? His cliff experience ended with the realization that "The Lord, God *had* shown His glory and His majesty" (Deut. 5:23). Helpless, he had to be assisted and guided to Damascus. He was blind for three days. This was a time of reconsideration, repenting and rebirth. Hearing from the Lord meant that he had to make a decision. Praying and seeing visions, Saul waited to receive the Holy Spirit and baptism. Once he regained his sight, Saul began preaching that Jesus is the Son of God despite persecution from the many who were not convinced. He was viewed as an apostate from Judaism. His name was changed to Paul. Following his moment of decision on the cliff, a paradox developed. The persecutor became the persecuted. One of the most energetic and tenacious figures of that day in the fight against Christianity, became a fighter in the spread of *the Way* rather than fighting to resist it.

The cliff experience has the invaluable trait of uncertainty. We cannot know the entire worth of any experience at the moment it is happening. There is no way of knowing the exact eventual outcomes of upcoming events. We can never know if that which makes us cry now, will bring a future blessing or whether the incident which causes much pain or suffering could bring edification and future rejoicing. Life's sorrows are opportunities to cooperate with God. Only time will reveal the true worth of our cliff experience. Since we do not have all wisdom and knowledge, as we go through struggles we may not recognize the benefit. Negative circumstances can have positive results. It does not require much faith at the edge of the cliff if the reward is known. For it is written:

> Christ has introduced us to God's undeserved kindness on which we take our stand. So we are happy, as we look forward to sharing in the glory of God. But that is not all! We gladly suffer, because we know that suffering helps us to endure. And endurance builds character, which gives us a hope that will never disappoint us. All of this happens because God has given us the Holy Spirit, who fills our hearts with His love. Rom. 5:2-5, CEV

We sometimes grow confused by life's contradictions—peace through storms, comfort through suffering, life through death, glory through shame. It is encouraging to know that Jesus Christ is Lord of all, even of that which appears unorthodox. He causes the world to take notice, bringing good out of bad and strength out of weakness. At the mountain's edge, one peers over to a level below that cannot be discerned, but descent is necessary, requiring faith and patience; and the choices made upon that crest determines how we mature spiritually.

A Crisis of Faith

> *Multitudes, multitudes in the valley of decision: for the day of the Lord is near in the valley of decision.*
>
> Joel 3:12

The enlightenment of knowing God through Jesus Christ discloses the reality of He who is invisible; The Great I AM. Whenever forced with life's decisions people think that the substance of the matter rests with their momentary circumstances. We contemplate what appears to be most important and that which is, at the time, in need of closure. The reality is that the summit of the mountain is analogous to the valley of decision. Much like the biblical narrative of the valley of Jehoshaphat, the cliffhanger is a turning point in history. A crisis of faith was represented when tumultuous times presented a national uprising against the Israelites. Their faith was tested. King Jehoshaphat stood at the cliff fearful, compromised, uncertain, and in need of guidance. As he pondered the available actions for this revolt, he reflected upon previous choices that may have led to this predicament and how altered circumstances may have created this new situation. He sought God for help. Most significant to his cliff experience is his relationship with God. The earnest beseeching prayer of King Jehoshaphat regarding the looming battle illustrates a reality for all Believers that "we have no might against this that comes against us; neither know what to do: but *we must keep* our eyes upon God knowing that the battle is the Lords, *not our own*" (I Chr.20:1-14; *emphasis mine*). Since all battles are being fought in the spiritual realm, during times of contemplation Satan seeks to attack the Believer's relationship with God causing doubt, fear, feelings of abandonment and inability. Once the child of God accepts relationship with Him this results in actions to serve Him and His righteousness which is displeasing to the world and havoc erupts on the mountain. No longer guided by the principles of the world the Believer does not wrestle with divided interest between allegiance to God and allegiance to Satan. Jesus said, "In the world you will have tribulation, but be of good cheer, I have overcome the world" (John 16:33). People often refer to great emotion-filled times of spiritual highs as mountaintop experiences and times in the valley are described as spiritually low periods. Although the cliffhanger cannot be classified as a low point in life, very few rejoice there. Because it is impossible to fully give oneself in two directions, preference is given to one or the other. The tension worsens when Christians forget their Creator and that it is He who owns the decision. Herein lies the contradiction expressed as a crisis of faith.

Everyone experiences a crisis of faith in their lifetime. We experience a crisis of faith when that special someone says they "don't love you anymore, when you hear from your superior that "your services at this organization are no longer required," and when the doctor says" it is malignant or we have done all we can." It also occurs when, like Peter, the child of God apparently confident in faith, hears Jesus say "come!" (Mat. 14:27-33) After many days of following Jesus, being obedient and learning from Him, Peter one of His disciples requested permission to venture out of the boat they were traveling in, onto the water with Jesus. The boat offered a semblance of safety and security. It was much more practical to be in the boat on the water than to stand on the water without the boat as he was suggesting. The courage of Peter to take the initial step over the side of the boat had to be remarkable to his onlookers. The absurdity of this situation is that the whole nature of man screams against this undertaking. The crisis of faith for most people is to abhor the initial step of faith although "the Spirit testifies with our spirit that we are children of God" (Rom. 8:16). Hearing the Lord's voice and attempting to ignore it, we make excuses, deny that it occurred and dismiss God's call or any internal aspiration as irrational. Peter left the boat, and walking on the surface of the water went toward Jesus (Mat. 14:29-30). He was willing to accept the call of Jesus without any thought of consequences. He braved the mountain and there at its peak his reason and rational mind began to contradict his courage. Suddenly, his faith is tested and he is faced with a crisis of faith. There at the edge of the cliff, Peter becomes afraid because familiarity with experience and theory in the natural overwhelms faith. What was he thinking to step out of the boat? How did he think he could stay afloat? Is Jesus really able to hold him up? His relationship with God is evident as Peter immediately calls out to Him. His relationship with God was not tested. What he understood about their relationship was tested. It is apparent that in those moments of decision the courage to trust God is critical and what we choose has consequences on spiritual growth.

The author of a favorite hymn, "It is Well with My Soul," had a memorable mountain journey which led to a crisis of faith. I am obliged to relay the cliff experience of Horatio G. Spafford, a well-known Chicago lawyer and businessman as written by Christine

Schaub.[12] In the 1860's, his was considered by human standards, a successful life. He had a wife, five children, a lucrative legal career and substantial real estate holdings. He was also a man who believed in God. Here was a man that was rich, successful and Christian, who came face to face with a crisis of faith! Horatio Spafford suffered almost unimaginable personal tragedy. First, his only son was killed by scarlet fever at the age of four. One year later, fire destroyed all of his real estate. Two years later, his four daughters were drowned when the ship they were on collided with another while on vacation. His wife was miraculously spared as she floated unconscious on a piece of wood. Spafford's cliff experience was naturally a place of despair. Even Satan scrutinizes mankind's motives toward God asking, is it not easy to be faithful when there is abundance? (Job 1:10) Questions often arise regarding the love and mercy of God during inclement periods at the pinnacle of the mountain. Similar to Job, the Child of God is especially taken aback by suffering when regarded by others as good, God-fearing and Christ-like. Spafford's crisis of faith took him to the only place to find answers; the Word of God. There he found solace in the response of a Shunammite woman over the sudden death of her only child. Although "her soul was troubled within her" she maintained that *it was well* with her (II Kings 4:26, 27). Horatio Spafford stepped off the cliff revealing a man with unwavering trust in God. Undoubtedly, no one can predict this response or expect that all Believers would react the same, even in considerably less difficult circumstances. In a crisis of faith, our confirmation is in resting on the knowledge that God will sustain us as he has done for countless children of the Most High. So no matter the situation, whether the outcome is good or bad, at the cliffs edge our spiritual man is engaged and developed.

Faith is often defined as trust or belief. The Bible states that "faith is given by God"(Rom. 12:3). "It is the substance of things hoped for and the evidence of things not seen" (Heb. 11:1-2). Scripture contends that faith is more than intellectual assent to certain beliefs. Faith is concerned with future intangible unseen events. Yet, faith is an expression of the Believer's relationship with God and confidence in His promises. To the unbelieving world, a God-honoring faith is illogical, nonsensical and unpopular. Such faith is wrought with temptation, suffering and persecution of various forms because it is beyond human understanding. One's faith is tested at the top of the mountain on the edge of the cliff. Here children of God give credence to their belief in the very existence of God. At stake is witness to His faithfulness and His sovereignty in the Believer's life because God's love is a confirmed reality as we live by faith. At the edge of the cliff, the individual must make a conscious and deliberate decision. During a crisis of faith, the child of God must decide whether to take God at His word, live expectantly and act obediently under the guidance of the Holy Spirit or to simply identify with the beliefs and practices of Christianity while contemplating and surrendering to the empirical elements of the natural world. A crisis of faith occurs when life events appear to contradict trusted values and beliefs. Comprehension about the things of God becomes muddied by life circumstances to challenge confidence in God's love and character. A crisis of faith may be described as a time when things in one's life do not make sense and the only rationale for continued existence is faith in God. Belief in His Word is what keeps the person from falling into despair, disparaging fear and hopelessness. As some individuals confront their crisis of faith the question of God's predetermined plan for mankind becomes the principle needed to comprehend life. A crisis of faith demands re-evaluation, reaffirmation and reconciliation to enable the Believer to address the conflict and advance on life's journey. The tension of the crisis of faith necessitates an uncompromising decision at the mountain summit as the end result. The cliffhanger experience is demonstrated as a crisis of faith when faced with intense doubts, disbelief and internal conflict regarding one's system of faith or an essential life decision. Considering that faith is a central tenet of religion, the concept of a crisis of faith is most commonly applied to those with religious beliefs. However, encountering doubt over influential life decisions such as choosing a marriage partner, treatment for an illness or relocation for a career proposes a time of consideration for humanity; and the acknowledgment of one's lack of absolute control causes a yielding to faith. It is here that there are questions about the rationality of life and faith. A relationship with God elicits the recognition that both life and faith originate from Him. Therefore, this relationship of faith is paramount to alleviating the stress of the cliffhanger, while the cliffhanger of necessity produces change in an individual's spiritual maturity.

But when we are judged, we are disciplined by the Lord so that we will not be condemned along with the world.

I Cor. 11:32

CHAPTER THREE

A Call to Consequence of Conviction

Jesus told His disciples "Do not suppose that I have come to bring peace to the earth. I did not come to bring peace, but a sword" (Mat. 10:34). The divisive nature of God's sword, which is Jesus, the Word of God and the message of the Gospel, presents as both gracious and cruel; and both nurturing and daunting (John 1:1). The "sword" is the means of dividing and separating the people of Christ from the men of the world and from their principles and practices. It is a means of dividing one relation from another with all of the separation, discord, and persecution arising from it and doctrinal truths from false teachings which has wrought dissensions within the body of Christ. Although not advocating that it was the intention and design of Christ's coming into the world to rouse and encourage such things but, through the malice and wickedness of men, this was eventually the effect and consequence of His coming. The word sword is used because the sword as a weapon divides unquestionably, as does the sword of the Spirit, the Word of God (Luke 12:51). The cliff experience can remind us that the "sword" is identified as having a *double-edge* (Heb. 4:12). Not only dividing and separating but granting its bearer power simply by wielding it. It is a weapon that commands proper handling which is spiritual obedience and as you become more familiar you grow more trusting of it. The Sword offers protection from harm, deliverance from mediocrity and the assurance of salvation. The Sword, as Jesus wielding the Word of God said, "It is finished; Into your hands I commit my spirit" and after that "the veil of the temple was torn in two" allowing Believers entrance to an individual crucifixion and resurrected life (Luke 23:45-46; John 19:30). The beauty of the Sword is that it has consigned us as new creatures in Christ and securely places us above the strongholds of this world. The sword of God commands unconditional surrender which presents as the initial consequence of conviction for Believers. Upon acceptance of the Gospel message through faith and receipt of the Holy Spirit, the Lord offers constraint of the individual's natural tendencies. The conscious and the subconscious of the child of God are quickened, necessitating choice between conflicting perspectives. For example, things that were so easy to do or say now result in hesitation or withdrawal. As faith heightens there is an endearing relationship with concern for God's perspective rather than one's own. This faith means that the person is unaware of actual anticipated events yet, is instructed by the Holy Spirit to persevere; and to trust and believe that every outcome will be God's best (Heb. 11:1).

The end-result in the purposes of God is what matters most. However, the journey which involves many choices and decisions affect the end-result. The uncertainties of the decision or outcome are another consequence of conviction and to respond antagonistically to the summons of God produces the consequence of conviction identified as repercussion. Jonah was a prophet of God. He had been known to prophesy to the chosen people of Israel during the reign of King Jereboam II. Commissioned by God to entreat the pagan nation of Nineveh to repent and receive salvation, Jonah attempted to escape God's calling by sailing from Joppa to Tarshish; as if God could not find him there. Jonah was convicted in his knowledge of God as Israel's Lord and equally evidenced conviction against those outside of their chosen people. The Ninevites had committed atrocities against the chosen people of Israel. Jonah would have liked to see them punished. Without repentance the Ninevites would suffer the consequences of their wickedness. He knew God as compassionate and loving but thought the Ninevites were unworthy to receive this attention from God. So Jonah decided to set sail in the opposite direction. The boat was assailed by tumultuous winds and waves. The passengers, aware of Jonah's conviction to disobedience, had to deliver Jonah's repercussion by throwing him overboard. God used a great fish to deliver Jonah to the Ninevites (1:17). He could have allowed the consequence of Jonah's conviction to oppose Him but God spared Jonah's life. The Book of Jonah, a section of the Old Testament, demonstrates that God has always desired the salvation of all people. But the prophet Jonah did not agree and standing at the edge of the cliff he was faced with a dilemma. Do I have a heart like the heart of God? Once I refuse, how do I return to the good graces of God? How can I inform outsiders of God's love? It is unimaginable that they should be treated like the Jewish people, Israel. Jonah did deliver the message of God. The people of Nineveh repented and were not destroyed. Jonah sulked because of this, still God showed compassion toward him. Jonah presents characteristics of bigotry, self-centeredness and ethnocentrism. He regarded God as exclusive property specific to one believing community. Fear and pride caused him to run from God. During his experience at the mountaintop his initial disobedience manifested the consequence of conviction leading, not only to personal restoration, spiritual growth and development, but the restoration and renewal of the Ninevites. All decisions have repercussions and decisions which appear to be in opposition of God's directives can still bring favor. Although there are certain repercussions from the natural world that comes with obedience to God, He gives "incomprehensible peace and unspeakable joy" to the one who endures (Phil. 4:7; I Pet. 1:8).

In the realm of the consequence of conviction we must consider emotion. Up on the mountain feelings, emotions and sensibilities are very important in our search for relevance, meaning and right choices in decision-making. Decision making is a cognitive process where the result is a choice between alternatives. According to psychologists, emotions are a dominant characteristic of our humanity. This fact means that it is necessary to identify and manage our emotions. Without the proper channeling emotions can wreak havoc on our circumstances as they usurp reasoning and effect *a disconnect* in positive spiritual growth. Every person has specific concerns. Proverbs 14:10 states, "the heart knows its own bitterness." There are issues, situations and circumstances of considerable difficulty for some while others can find contentment. There are many factors which influence feelings, making them variable. Research exposes the values, benefits and difficulties that emotions present to decision-making. Psychology and other mental and emotional health literature suggests that totally emotional decisions are typically fast and that rational thinking takes longer depending on the degree of logic included in the process. Even within a spiritual perspective, where the Believer acknowledges the promptings of God, it is the nature of man to wrestle with pros and cons; bearing in mind the emotional and logical remedy. Instead, during these instances, the main driving force should be knowledge of God's Word, wisdom through experience, answered prayer and faith. Additionally, scientists and scholars have reported that when identifying spiritual choices, it is in reference to decisions that *feel or seem right*. They categorize these descriptors as signals from the subconscious. Many individuals make the terrible mistake of allowing feelings to be the central focus when making decisions. Emotions are volatile. This is especially noticeable when emotions are central in the decision-making process. Emotional responses keep the focus on the individual; Holy Spirit responses keep the focus on God. Considering the variability of feelings it necessitates the importance of reflection, meditation and prayer when confronting choices. Scripture reminds us to be concerned about the things of God and what has His approval (Mat. 6:33). When people use logic to make decisions there is an attempt to exclude emotions. Using logic or emotions to discover spiritual truths should be avoided. Here again the individual's perspective is the driving force for truth. Accordingly, truth is fashioned by culture, tradition and environment.

> For those who are according to the flesh set their minds on the things of the flesh, but those who are according to the Spirit, the things of the Spirit. The mind set on the flesh is hostile toward God; for it does not subject itself to the law of God, for it is not even able *to do so*, and those who are in the flesh cannot please God. Rom. 8:5-8

God has given particular commandments which can help decision making, so, if a specific course of action is contrary to the teachings in His Word, then it is not God's will in the matter. The Word of God contends that the spiritual things of God are comprehensible only by the spirit (I Cor. 2:14-15). Emotional responses to the cliff experience often render a demand for reciprocity. Much like the discourse of Peter who, disavowing the principle of grace, asked Jesus what the disciples would receive in return for their loyalty to Him. Jesus informed him that "many who are first will be last and the last first" (Matt. 19:30). Emotions heighten expectations. The perspective is that one deserves or is entitled. When decisions are warranted emotions are often incited when disclosure is limited. Jesus told a parable about a landowner hiring employees for the day (Mat. 20:1-16). In the parable the workers began to murmur and complain that some of them had received harsh treatment. They displayed feelings of contempt towards others, which manifests as we become more self-centered than God-centered. The workers perceived that the landlord had misled them although they received what had been promised. Emotions guided their decision making, and their choices were demonstrated by aberrant behaviors. Ascribing unrighteousness to God causes an inability to leave the mountain. Emotions are an affront at the crest of the mountain. They may cause mistakes in decision making by distorting truths and creating bias in judgment. Projected emotions can lead to errors that override reasonableness. As doubt, fear and double-mindedness prevail, spiritual growth is thwarted. Emotions in tuned with the Holy Spirit function to balance reasoning which results in opportunity to evaluate our assignment more fully under the microscope of God's Word. Despite the conviction of emotions our time on the cliff is the call of God to relationship where we "learn what He is about to do where we are."[13] So like Elijah, let us make an emotional plea to the Most High saying, "Today let it be known that you are God and I am your servant and I have done all things at thy word" (I King 18:36).

Finally, the call to consequence of the mountain top experience brings distinction. Each Christian is an individual, created by God, who has been restored by His grace and distinguished as different. This distinction represents that the child of God has made a necessary choice which has recognizable behaviors notable as sanctification unto Him, distinct from the normative carnal response to life. The Word of God asserts that surrender, outcome, repercussion and distinction mold the lives of the children of God. The choice "to take up your cross and follow Christ" is acknowledged as a process of distinction (Luke 9:23). As the exemplary servant of the Lord, Jesus carried out his mission in solidarity, in service and under the humiliation of death on a cross. He presented without fanfare and did not fit the natural model of humanity. The servant leader could not be understood with the standardized logic of success and power used by the world. On earth to fulfill the will of the Father, Jesus carried out his mission of salvation. For the Believer to take up their cross and follow Christ is faith. A sacrifice that is the evidence of which the Bible speaks (Heb.11:1). It is demonstrably proof of love, signifying a radical choice where there is no hesitation or second thoughts. It is a demanding obligation that disconcerted even the disciples who witnessed Jesus' life. Even today these words are regarded as a stumbling block and foolishness (I Cor. 1: 22-25). But, we have to choose, because although the circumstances and situations of the world do not depend on us, our life depends on the decisions we make and other lives do, too. The consequence of conviction is demonstrated by responsiveness to the calling and required task of God. Each person must choose between two distinct alternatives: what God says do and what you as the individual believe that you should do. During the cliff experience, since the natural instinct is often the choice to follow one's own mind instead of the Holy Spirit, there is disappointment, heartache and confusion. Still, toward the child of God, He is merciful. We must remember that our calling is not simply to establish our own personal relationship with God but it is to introduce all nations to Him. God spares us from the many times our convictions create consequence. To be obedient and to be ready to accept the plan of God depends upon each of us. God does not ask us to give up living, but to accept the newness and a fullness of life that only He can give. Human beings have a tendency to self-centeredness; to regard oneself as the standard against which to gauge everything. Carrying the cross does not refer primarily to the need to endure patiently the great and small tribulations of life, or, the exaltation of pain as a means of pleasing God. It means being united with Him through faith and offers the greatest proof of love. When we speak about the cross it carries the distinction of God's love for us. When the cross is embraced it becomes a sign of love, peace, hope and of total self-giving bringing distinction to Christianity. A Christian's acceptance encourages examination of the natural world relative to the purposes of God warranting essential decisions and actions consistent with His will embodying distinction. It shapes our spirituality, directs our identity and aims our way of life.

The Sword Divides Asunder

And if it is with difficulty that the righteous is saved, what will become of the godless man and the sinner?

I Peter 4:18

The consequence of conviction is unconditional surrender. "Do you love me more than these? Jesus asked" (John 21:15). This question is at the central point of discipleship and reveals a person's heart. Our decisions at the cliff are based on these premises. What do we love the most? Have we abandoned all to follow Jesus? With every cliffhanger these questions are raised. Every time we become preoccupied with the good that God provides us these questions are raised. Then, Jesus says, deny yourself and others who have set themselves apart from God and follow Me (Mat. 10:37; 12:48; 16:24). This reveals Jesus' bringing the disciples, particularly Peter, more completely under his lordship. Jesus' questioning goes deeper than the issue of superficial affirmations. He brings attention to lust at the root of sin. Notwithstanding the commonplace definition, lust is being enthralled with selfish motives marked by the underpinnings of lack of control. We are to surrender to God the insatiable desires of the natural man which is "to do what seems right in *our* own eyes" (Judges 21:25). Although the Bible rejects disunity and division as opposing the very nature of God, it characterizes the Word of God as the sword which will ultimately, of necessity, bring division. Its contention is that "no man can serve two masters: for either he will hate the one, and love the other; or else he will hold to the one, and despise the other" (Mat.6:24). Its blade of truth is applied to reveal the soul and spirit of man. The sword separates and makes the pursuit of God's purposes possible as the Holy Spirit guides mankind's examination of the evidence enabling judgment to reason through the senses. This leads to "equipped saints for the work of service until we all attain to the unity of the faith, and of the knowledge of the Son of God, to a mature man, to the measure of the stature which belongs to the fullness of Christ" expressed in obedience as unconditional surrender.

Life is full of hard choices between less than perfect alternatives and the unknown circumstances of the future. Your life has been filled with many bad choices. For you, life has been one problem after another; a vicious spiral. When you think that you have sunk as low as you can go, you come to another sublevel. At every twist and turn on life's road you believe that just around the corner is everything you have hoped for. You say, "Things will be better. This time I will try harder. I will not give in; besides this road looks a little easier." Suddenly, as if out of nowhere, you find yourself, not only back where you started from but, worse than you were; and it seems that you are never quite sure how it happens (Mat. 12:44-45). Since you have no recollection, then you cannot be at fault; or maybe you do recall something. Nevertheless, your bad situation is caused by someone else. Now, of course, you don't mean that you did not get that speeding ticket for speeding, the DUI for driving intoxicated, land in jail for stealing, fighting, killing or whatever the case may be. No, you actually performed the act, but, the reason for your action is the fault of someone else. It is like a revolving door going around in circles. Just think of how many people on this earth have come to the same conclusion. How many of them never choose to think differently in order to act differently and escape the revolving door. To escape you must step off the cliff into what appears an abyss. You have heard of faith but you believe in fate, and feel that you have just not been as lucky as other people. Now, standing at the edge, you realize that you must choose to believe so that you can escape and take control of your life. You must believe in a faith which declares: to expect positive things to come from positive actions. Although these positive things may not happen following several attempts of positive actions, faith means that you surrender and keep anticipating that sooner rather than later they will happen. This is a faith that empowers and promotes long-term changes in lifestyle and behavior to result in victory over what has seemed to be insurmountable challenges. Stepping off is initiated when you take responsibility and accept that you are accountable for your own life. This first step is the precursor to spiritual maturity. Now your life is no longer spiraling, but has a new direction through unconditional surrender; and the revolving door stops to allow you an exit to your future.

In the Book of Genesis we find the narrative regarding Isaac's sons, Esau and Jacob; twins whom the Bible introduces as jostling with each other even in the womb (Gen. 25:22). From the beginning, Jacob emerges as one striving for personal advantage. As with most children born into the same family, each young man matured as very different individuals; Esau, the firstborn son, as "a skillful hunter, a man of the field and Jacob, as a mild man, dwelling in tents" (Gen. 25:27). Jacob would later become known as Israel, which means one who struggles with God (spiritual things) while Esau would struggle with men and animals (natural things). Both demonstrated natural human character flaws. The entire human race is flawed in some way or another as the Bible affirms: the natural man is a sinner who falls short and has a heart that is desperately wicked (Rom. 3:23; Jer.17:9). However, people are called to be prudent in making choices; choosing God and His strengths over human weaknesses and maintaining His moral vision. The report of Esau's defeat implies failed choices based on the unreliable aspects of the instinctual motivation of man. Jacob demonstrated his wiles as he recognized an advantage and pursued it by bartering and acquiring Esau's birthright for a bowl of lentil stew. The birthright encompasses a family ranking of distinction and a larger portion of inheritance. Esau did not honor his birthright. He was detached or disinterested regarding it. Who would not expect that a birthright would be retained forever, since it is based upon a God-determined birth order? Esau apparently regarded his birthright as *of little worth*. His choice to exchange it for a momentary pleasure reveals his struggle between the natural man and the purposes of God. Who would trade a bowl of stew for their inheritance? Who would discount their future for the immediacy of the moment, today? Many people do and it is often due to the limited perspective of humanity. This limited ego-centric point of view thwarts the spiritual growth that is paramount to the cliffhanger experience. Standing at the cliff's edge with decisions to make, we are often misguided by "the lust of the flesh, the lust of the eyes and the boastful pride of life:" personal desires, instant gratification, cultural norms or societal pressures (I John 2:16). The Bible presents a very different resolution to decision making. It says, "trust in the Lord with all of your heart and lean not to your own understanding" (Prov. 3:5). Our understanding is fallible. Since every decision brings consequence we must be mindful to acknowledge the Lord first and he will guide our efforts toward understanding (Prov. 3:6). The cliffhanger requires unconditional surrender as a consequence of conviction to impart spiritual development. For the Sword, God's Word, is capable of dividing that which could never be separated otherwise. It is powerful and penetrating (Heb. 4:12). "Those far stronger than you have fallen beneath its power" (Ezek. 21:10, NKJV).

Bear Fruit

> *I will go to the great and will speak to them, for they know the way of the LORD and the ordinance of their God." But they too, with one accord, have broken the yoke and burst the bonds.*
>
> Jeremiah 5:5

The consequence of conviction is repercussion. Christ has created His body of Believers to work together as a team, where diverse people have varied gifts and utilize these gifts to benefit each other. Scriptures promise is that all Believers are children of God and therefore heirs to the spiritual inheritance and in Christ have something to offer to build up the kingdom. Though it can be overwhelming trying to determine where the Lord would have you serve His body, knowing and acknowledging the gifting which He has provided helps to place your focus in the right direction and assists with ascertaining the ministry in which you will be most effective. The spiritual gifts along with passion, abilities, personality and experience makes fulfillment possible as you endeavor to bear fruit. The body of Christ has been fashioned as an organized group with individual qualities necessary for the "equipping of the saints for works of service" in the effective functioning for the advancement of God's kingdom (Eph. 4:12). The local assemblies, whether recognized consecrated sanctuaries or fields of grass have been ordained and established by God for the teaching and preparing of every saint to perform their God assigned task. "For we are God's workmanship, created in Christ Jesus to do good works, which God prepared in advance for us to do" (Eph. 2:10). Although knowing that the body of Christ has a universal membership, congregations around the globe find themselves struggling with the familial relationship of saints outside of their local or identified assembly. This has been established according to tradition of men as divisions, false teachings and arguments regarding genealogies, days, food, and feasts which are unacceptable in the purposes of God (I Tim. 1:4; Titus 3:8; Rom. 14:5-6; I Cor. 8:8). The role of genealogy and tradition has a place in providing a lens through which to understand one's familial history, its subsequent characteristics, relations and cultural norms. They can strengthen relations and reinforce values and self-image. However, both have been noted to cause dissension within families and between friends. The same has been identified with establishing special days, food and feasts. Traditions, genealogies, days, food, and feasts have recognized benefit in contributing to community and yet, are a repercussion that can have a detrimental impact as they instigate negativity to the point of utter disregard for the foundational commandment of God to love one another.

A traditional viewpoint is contrary to the perspective of God. As we aspire to be religious, we lose the substance that God demands. Even in Jesus' day He attempted to redirect the religious groups from being law and tradition centered to being centered in love and the expansion of Truth. In the Book of Mark, Jesus rebukes the Scribes and Pharisees for placing their traditions above the commands of God. Traditions are noted as regular activities or rituals performed to enrich life, instruct, and guide. These may also be observed as strict rules or guidelines, old outdated patterns of behavior or endeavors stifling inspiration. There was conflict between Jesus and the prevalent religious sects. The Pharisees accused Jesus and His disciples of violating the sacred traditions. They could not understand how Jesus, a practicing Jew, would not observe their religious customs, policies and practices. They determined that His actions were improper and sought to kill Him. Jesus' response was not to disavow the traditions but to establish that the Believer ascertain the reason for observing them. Even today this necessitates determining whether the tradition causes displacement of loyalty, magnifies one's own self-righteousness or demonstrates betrayal of the fundamental nature of God's Word. Our minds and hearts must be in line with the foundational reason for the tradition otherwise, as Jesus contends, we act as hypocrites (Mark 7:6). What good are special days, feasts and rituals if they exclude the foundational message of God? God's foundational message is left out as mankind waivers between tradition, genealogy, culture and societal norms; and the command of His Word to love Him above all else and one another. Jesus inferred that the religious people of His day were *old wineskins* holding to the natural inclinations of religious customs and traditions of men rather than the evidence of God. "You cannot put new wine into old wineskins" (Mark 2:22). According to the Bible, we are required to put aside natural inclinations and progress forward for a *higher* prize (Phil. 3:13-14).

The Book of Esther presents a mountain experience suggesting disregard for tradition, culture and societal norms. Esther, a young orphaned Jewish girl, was raised by her cousin, Mordecai who worked for the king of Persia. She was among the women ordered to be brought to the palace when the king sought to replace his wife after she humiliated him. Esther was chosen by the king to be his queen. Haman, a prominent man in the kingdom, devised a scheme to destroy the entire Israelite community by decree of the king. When the decree was announced to the masses, Mordecai sent a message to Queen Esther telling her to go to the king and plead for her people. What a task for this young woman! The king did not know she was Jewish. "Mordecai had warned her not to tell anyone that she was a Jew, and she obeyed him" (Esth. 2:10). When she first learned of Haman's plot and threat to the existence of the Jewish people, Esther demonstrated helplessness. By law, anyone who entered the inner court to approach the king without permission was to be put to death and she had not been summoned in many days, which could imply that she had fallen from favor (Esth. 4:11). This experience at the cliff's edge directed her thoughts and concerns to question: her status as the queen, her relationship to the king, the repercussion of not obeying the laws and traditions; and her position as a chosen vessel in God's kingdom. Had God elevated Esther to the role of queen for the purpose of helping to save her people? (Esth. 4: 13-14) Did God really want her to die? If she refused to help the Jews would God allow her to die? Would He forgive her if she refused? Could she refuse to help and allow the entire Jewish community to be annihilated? She had to give Mordecai an answer. Although consumed with tension and anxiety she initiated intercessory and corporate prayer and fasting amongst the brethren (Esth. 4:15-16).

At the edge of her cliff she realized her purpose in life was to fulfill the task set before her; saying, "If I perish, I perish" (4:16). Esther placed her life in the hands of God and allowed Him to decide the outcome. She ignored much more than the natural concerns of tradition, genealogy, law, culture and societal expectations, she even discounted her own life for the assignment that she had been given. The mountain affords each Believer the opportunity to learn of God, to find peace in times of decision on the cliff's edge and to cast their concerns upon Him knowing that He cares (Mat. 11:29; I Pet. 5:7). The Bible depicts many occasions when an individual relied on God to be that rock of habitation to which we may continually come, and He delivered them from difficulty (Ps.71:3). He is in control, for it is written:

> If the Lord had not been my help, My soul would soon have dwelt in *the abode of* silence. If I should say, "My foot has slipped, "Your loving-kindness, O Lord, will hold me up. When my anxious thoughts multiply within me, Your consolations delight my soul. (Psalm 94:17-19)

At the edge of the cliff, the choice to accept that God is real, all-powerful and promises to always be with you must be understood and believed (Heb. 13:5). Each final outcome is always decided by Him. Letting go of traditional thinking and cultural norms is never easy, as witnessed, in the books on the Gospel, by the incessant discourse regarding laws, customs and traditions between Jesus and the religious leaders; until they put the Son of God to death. The natural inclination is to experience displeasure relative to change. Sometimes the displeasure is so overwhelming that the character of Jesus, God's messenger of love, which is to be made manifest in the lives and behaviors of Christians is arrested. The repercussion is that the conduct that God approves is replaced by cynicism, condescension and other forms of satanic attack. In our spiritual world the consequence of conviction means loyalty to God and His Word in opposition to the normative concepts and precepts persistently held by the natural mind of the physical world. While God is working things out behind the scenes it is necessary for spiritual growth, to seek His will irrespective of the way things have always been done.

Through each cliffhanger experience, children of God grow in effectiveness for the purpose of God as they overcome their dilemmas through confident decision making based on the life of Jesus, the Holy Spirit and His Word.

Distinction

We are the true circumcision, who worship in the Spirit of God and glory in Christ Jesus and put no confidence in the flesh
Phil. 3:3

Who do people say that I am? The consequence of conviction is distinction. As Christians, our distinction is that we have direct access to His Majesty; the King of Kings. Standing in the shadow of the cross, we bow our head to pray and worship God; and His Spirit intercedes through our mental and emotional perplexity. Our uniqueness in God's purpose is revealed by our assigned spiritual gifts, personality, innate talents, developed temperament and acquired skills. These distinguishing features, and our physical attributes, determine our distinction in the plan of God. As we learn, understand and accept our design, we are made markedly useful to the Kingdom. Until then, we can lead seemingly haphazard lives, finding ourselves most frequently involved as the main character of a cliffhanger. Every aspect of our lives can become suspenseful, starting with melodramatic episodes having uncertain results, followed by abrupt endings to discover ourselves in yet, another precarious situation. The mistakes we have made become insignificant compared to the significance of time, space and its continuum in God. Ironically, spiritual growth entails adversity, sadness, trials, frustrations, loss and suffering. All of these apparently hurtful situations should lead us to one place at the pinnacle. With our heart's desire centered on the God who holds yesterday, today and tomorrow. Jesus asked His disciples what people were saying about Him. Their answers varied. Then He asked who do you, *who are called by my name,* say that I am? Simon Peter answered, saying, "You are the Christ, the Son of the living God; Jesus answered and said to him "blessed are you, for flesh and blood has not revealed this to you"

Mat. 16:15-17). Identification with the person of Jesus Christ as Lord and Savior elicits a profoundly personal bond. "Who shall bring any charge against God's elect? It is God who justifies" (Rom.8:33). This statement asserts that the relationship between God and His children is intimate giving them distinction. The depth of this relationship leads the Believer to lose interest in selfish individuality, to become confidently devoted to God through Jesus Christ. The experience of the cliffhanger can cause the individual to contemplate that there is no hope of deliverance in human wisdom. The decision to trust God at this summit and to surrender means that I believe I am who He says that I am. This decision is the absolute cure for spiritual apathy, doubt, disbelief or deterioration. Discovering our ineptness, accepting our unworthiness and giving God prominence as primary for living, we achieve confidence in Him, realize our distinctiveness, grow because of His grace and gain the reassurance of who we may become through Him.

In the Book of Judges, chapters 13-16, we discover Samson who was a judge in Israel. He was famous for his strength and the prowess he displayed against the Philistines. The name Samson, in Hebrew means distinguished. Prior to his birth, his mother was informed that he had been ordained by God to live differently from the other Hebrew children. He was dedicated to God as a Nazarene from birth. A Nazarene was consecrated to the Lord by lifestyle and a special vow (Num. 6). Samson was separated to God but, could never come to terms with his sanctification. "He willingly disobeyed God, practiced deceit, gave way to temper and vindictiveness and dallied with evil"[14] From a young age Samson desired women who honored different gods, despite knowing that this was in opposition to his destiny. He was intent to follow his personal desires rather than heed his purpose in the plan of God. Many children of God struggle with knowing their purpose. There are those who know what God has called them to do but struggle with accepting and living their purpose, and there are others who disregard it altogether. Samson appears arrogantly defiant as he defiles himself by eating honey from a carcass, drinking wine and fraternizing with the enemy of God (Num. 6:1-10). He lived his life with blatant disregard for the directives of God. He was wayward and unpredictable which is represented from the chosen people of the Old Testament to the Church of contemporary society. Samson's biblical narrative presents a cliffhanger where the main character suffers tragedy. He put his life into the hands of a treacherous woman who betrayed him causing his final separation from God, the loss of his strength, blindness by the hand of his enemy, imprisonment and death. Here was a man who totally and unashamedly separated himself from God, who had given him power and favor. Still, he was God's chosen vessel with an assignment to liberate the nation of Israel, so in spite of him, this would not be hindered. Although things and people appear to be out of control, the all-knowing Lord uses these individuals and circumstances to achieve his purposes. Samson, like many of us at our cliff, realized his failures, cried out to the Lord, acknowledged his weakness and total need of God (Num. 6:18-19). This man of distinction fulfilled his mission at the cost of his life. Would he have been so undisciplined had he known the price to be paid? Was the price due to his determined obstinacy toward God? His cliff experience demonstrates that the relationship between God and mankind is one of human liberty and God's Sovereignty. At one level there is a repulsive tale of retaliation and ever-escalating violence where actions are driven by dark forces. At another level it is Gods power resulting in victory over defeat; "a contrast of strength and weakness."[15] Much like Samson, who through his own shortcomings was given distinction as he demonstrated his spiritual capacities while carrying out God's will, so it is with every Believer. However, just as Samson was unaware of the future events of his own story, so every man is unaware. God doesn't often reveal his strategies or outcomes in His efforts of perfecting and purifying which, in the midst of our circumstances, may indeed seem incidental, yet all things happen according to His perfect will and timeline. The Word of the Lord is "if any man would come after me, let him deny himself; and take up his cross and follow Me" (Mark 8:34). This is most evident during our determined choices at the edge of the cliff. It is here that the testing of our faith and the significance of acting according to God's will takes place. *Upon this rock* your identity in Christ is fashioned. It is at the moment when dilemma confounds, circumstances dishevel and the noisy roar of life deafens, that the disciple learns faith within the meaning of the Master's commands to *follow Me* and is truly raised to a position of distinction.

How many times have you heard young folk say, "I cannot wait until I am an adult, then nobody can tell me what to do?" it is likely that over half as many think it than say it. At a time in your life, you may have been part of this statistic; now you are an adult. But in place of mom, dad and older siblings now, it is a boss, mate, co-worker or friend who is telling you what to do; and although you are aware that in many situations there is a need for authority, you cannot imagine, much less comprehend, that this applies to you. You think to yourself "I have been deciding for myself since I have been able to choose what clothes to wear." Even as an employee, if you are told the goals of the company and the objectives of the department you can manage yourself well enough to meet them. So far, you have found yourself at odds with every supervisor you have had. It appears to them that you are not a team player and cannot be directed. You are considered insubordinate and you emphatically deny this assessment. You are independent, and being independent you do what you want. You argue, "Why assemble a committee when you know what to do?" Besides, working alone is when you are happiest and can get the most accomplished. One day, while working, you decide to correct a situation that, you have decided, has the potential for disaster if not addressed immediately. You know the protocol is to contact your supervisor for guidance, but the urgency of the matter requires action. You reason that the supervisor will have you do the work anyway, so you take the initiative and do it on your own. The task is completed in no time flat and everyone is pleased, except your supervisor. For you, the decision to act may not be a cliffhanger. But in actuality, it is. The Bible states in James 4:17: "When one knows what is the right thing to do it is imperative to do the right thing." It never matters if you believe that you have the best objective for the desired outcome. Each situation includes separate and distinct persons with specific choices and decisions to be made within the scope of each issue. Every individual has a role that must be carried out as required by the context of the matter. Neither should be ignored or presumed to have the best idea for all concerned. The Bible contends that we treat others the way we want to be treated and to love our brother as we love ourselves (Luke 6:31; Mat. 22:39). If we do not, there will be consequences. In reference to your job, you never considered that there would be consequences. The situation called for an urgent response and you responded. With a worldly outlook, one not tempered by the love of God, independence often becomes self-aggrandizement. Now, you are before an irate supervisor who is faced with a crisis of their own. Your actions, though short-sighted, may have been beneficial; nevertheless your behavior does not supersede the hierarchy of the organization. Therefore, the supervisor has the authority to reprimand. If a relationship of communication had been established prior to this occurrence, your supervisor may have recognized your independence as an asset and welcomed your exceptional qualities, empowering you to handle the matter. But since a relationship of mutual respect had not occurred, honor and recognition for averting disaster is not forthcoming. Now you both are confronting the cliff. Standing at the cliff each individual must confront the heart of the matter; the inner man, where the intricacies of passion and lust are housed. The Word of God expresses that there is no hope of deliverance in human wisdom. We cannot allow personal effects, concepts, traditions and hierarchies to cause us to waiver away from who God says we are to be. God's truth reminds us to "Fear the LORD and do not join with the rebellious" (Prov. 24:21). We must examine the will of God for our lives declaring, "I am distinctly, who God says that I am in Jesus!" So then each one of us will give an account of himself to God; therefore let us not judge one another anymore, but rather determine not to put an obstacle or a stumbling block in a brother's way" (Rom. 14:13-13). As with every cliff experience, the ability to display your uniqueness as a child of God, the Creator, is based on there being a time for introspection, which can lead to spiritual growth.

Who has not heard of Moses? *Moses was educated in all the learning of the Egyptians* and the wisdom of ancient Egypt was unrivaled (I Kings 4:30; Acts 7:22). Egypt was also wealthy economically and distinguished by its advancements of the arts, architecture and the natural sciences. Its military prowess was unmatched and political governance renown. Moses knew a lot. The Bible says, he was "a man of power in words and deeds" (Acts 7:22). His life story begins in Egypt where a frightened king, fearing the loss of power and position, ordered the murder of all the Israelite boys that ranged in age of two and below. An Israelite woman placed her infant son into a woven basket and released it among the reeds of the Nile River. The king of Egypt's daughter discovered him, named him Moses and raised him as her own. "Moses was no ordinary child" (Acts 7:20, NIV). According to the biblical account, he was *exceedingly lovely.* Paradoxically, Moses, an Israelite, grew to adulthood in an Egyptian household. He was in line to become the pharaoh. At age forty, his conscience was provoked by the mistreatment of the Hebrew people and the normalcy of his life was threatened after he was observed killing an Egyptian who was beating a Hebrew slave (Ex. 2:11-12; Acts 7:23-25). This provided the motivation for his flight and ultimate sojourn in Midian where he received his commission from God. The compassionate, impulsive and confident Moses, Prince of Egypt, had to learn of God in the solitude of his mountain. Nothing was as he expected; the family he knew, neither the pharaoh he respected nor the community of Hebrews he supervised. God was introduced to Moses in Midian, it is humbling to learn the power of faith and to see the providence of God.

By faith Moses, when he had come of age, refused to be called the son of Pharaoh's daughter choosing to suffer affliction along with the people of God rather than enjoy the temporary pleasure of sin; esteeming "the reproach of the coming reward of Christ greater riches than the treasures of Egypt. By faith Moses, left Egypt, not fearing the wrath of the king; for he persevered, as seeing him who is invisible" (Heb. 11:24-27). For the next forty years Moses was content to remain in the land of Midian (Ex. 2:21). An aspect of his training on the mountain top was that his attention to his inadequacies was met with God's reassurances. Each of Moses' objections was centered on himself, demonstrating the frailty of human beings (Ex. 3:11-4:17). Moses' assignment brought him face to face with a major life-changing decision. His task was to deliver God's people from the Egyptians. He was commissioned by God to approach the most powerful man in the land to demand liberty for the Israelites. God's request was very disconcerting. Moses was a refugee from Egypt, a wanted felon who feared for his life, now, God commanded that he return there with demands. Surely God must have been jesting; and being conscious of all his faults, fears and failures, Moses attempted to dissuade the Lord. This appointment was too much. It was more than he was equipped to handle. How could he, with his speech impediment communicate for God? Moses had been in the position to rule all of Egypt. Egypt was the most powerful nation on earth at the time. He was hand-picked by God and positioned to give up the world's premier place of authority to lead God's people; a nation of slaves, to the Promised Land against the proud, unyielding, stern and cruel Egyptian ruler. There at the crest of the mountain, Moses resolved to obey God and through many signs and wonders the Lord established that He is able to make all that he has created effective for His purpose. Moses' faith in God increased. Paul states in II Corinthians 13:5 to "examine yourselves as to whether you are in the faith." Choices we face that seem indefinable, but could produce a positive outcome, should instill in us, with humility, a greater faith that God is working in us, through us and with us for His glory. The Word of God asserts that He diligently provides for our calling and salvation. Moses is given the distinction as the Hebrew who led the Israelites out of Egypt to freedom despite the odds and the one who delivered the Law of God during their years in the wilderness. His acknowledged relationship with God by faith and his effectual spiritual growth occurred as a consequence of conviction during his cliffhanger experience.

If the Lord is God, follow Him: but if Baal, then follow him.
I King 18:21

CHAPTER FOUR

A Call to Conflict

In this life there will be struggles, tribulations and conflicts. Conflict can be defined as difference, variance, inconsistency, incompatibility, clash and war. The Word of God portrays each of these descriptors by contrasting the incompatibility of law and grace, the difference in defeat and victory, the clash between reasoning and revelation, the inconsistency of bondage and freedom, the variance of cursing and blessing, and the war entangling living in the flesh and walking in the Spirit. Inwardly, the conflict of decision for an unregenerate humanity is whether one shall stand for upright honorable principles or depart from them, to secure an anticipated advantage. This may be a relentless conflict; however it is not to be considered as the conflict between the *flesh and the Spirit*, of which the Bible speaks. According to the Bible, "God is Spirit and those who worship Him must worship Him in spirit" (John 4:24). The motivation of the heart in which we worship him is most important and developed through a yielded relationship with Him whereby the Word of God is paramount; "for the Word of God is living, active and sharper than any two-edged sword, piercing as far as the division of soul and spirit, of both joints and marrow, and able to judge the thoughts and intentions of the heart" (Heb. 4:12). The writer of this verse provides the analogy that the Word of God is like a sword that is sharp enough to cut right through the outer, hard, tough part of a bone, into the inner soft living part of the bone. The depth of meaning in this analogy is that "who God is" and "who we are" in relation to Him, are revealed. There is the acknowledgment that God wants our intimacy. Intimacy can be defined as harmony and vulnerability without trespass or contempt. What often emerge are feelings of inadequacy, unworthiness and shame, in contrast to the Holy One who loves unconditionally; so we war in our spirit and with our soul against the desired intimacy of our God. This is the war that Paul reveals when he writes: "I find then a law, that evil is present with me, the one who wills to do good; for I delight in the law of God according to the inward man. But I see another law in my members, warring against the law of my mind, and bringing me into captivity to the law of sin which is in my members." (Rom. 7:21-23; NKJV). Some don't realize the conflict; that we are in a battle of spiritual supremacy and control. Individuals who are immersed in sin and dead to the truths of God's Word cannot feel this conflict; for them nothing opposes the flesh. The spiritual nature of God revealed by His Holy Spirit is considered an atrocity to the natural mind. Although the natural man struggles with conflict every day, which may be merely instinctual, sensual impulses and principles or circumstances of life which *press on every side*, their moment at the cliff is not the consequential conflict which exists in the heart of one who fears God. When the choice is made and the conflict ceases for the natural man, unavoidably it involves principle. This encompasses the individual consciousness of right or wrong behaviors and cultural, societal, and religious norms established as proper, and that are used in decision making. Whether it ends in the victory or the defeat of a better principle, it leaves the natural man just where it found him—under the power of sin and Satan, without God and without hope-still united to the world. How different is the conflict spoken of in God's Word for the Christian. Jesus, who has been tempted in all things as we are, yet without sin, is our means of escape if we accept Him (I Cor. 10:13). People are informed of the inevitability of conflict and are instructed to *walk by the Spirit* and to dissuade the desires of the flesh, "for the flesh sets its desire against the Spirit, and the Spirit against the flesh; for these are in opposition to one another" (Gal. 5:16-17). The spiritual man discovers that the conflict on the cliff elicits choice affecting the spiritual nature as well as the physical. Hebrews 4:14 reminds the Believer that we have a high priest who has experienced; and identifies with and understands, the conflicts of humanity. If we contemplate the experience, we may discover where we are along the mountain and be permitted a glimpse into the reason for our experience above the abyss. Therefore, spiritual maturity is influenced by responses to the conflict encountered along the journey and by decisions at the cliff for both the natural and the spiritual man.

Examples of this conflict are marked in the Bible from Genesis to Revelation portraying people at odds with God, within themselves, and with others. The cliffhanger's *call to conflict* is an illustration of the process and the price for intimacy with God and His family. Intimacy is achieved at the price of facing idiosyncrasies, understanding them and resolving them. Resolving them is prompted by a fear of God which is respect for His Sovereignty and acceptance of His love. For the heart that fears God, the conflict is the human nature being contested, consequently, when the Holy Spirit governs, conflict is abated and the Believer is made alive unto God. This is the result of spiritual conflict: a challenge for life or death where the old life dies and a new life emerges (II Cor. 5:17; Gal. 2:20). This conflict is known by the children of God experientially. The *call to conflict* evident at the cliff is an unceasing battle between natural law and God's grace; between the flesh and the Spirit. The reality is that the outcome of this conflict is not prolonged, vague or uncertain, as some maintain, for its end is present victory for eternity.

The *call to conflict*, which is affirmed throughout the Bible, is akin to the process of balancing a set of scales, a tangible apparatus in the natural realm, as one side gains weight or value, the other side loses weight or value. There is a comparable conflict in the spiritual realm. Without faith in God the world is controlled by chance and randomness. There is chaos with an emphasis on competition and acquisition. The individual often seeks to balance the tangible with the intangible; logic with luck, and for the Believer the spiritual with the natural. An individual cannot elevate both God and self. Jesus explained the impossibility of this effort saying "no one can serve two masters, either you will hate one and love the other or be devoted to one and despise the other" (Mat. 6:24). Many Christians neglect Jesus' teaching that Believers are to lay up treasures in heaven instead of concentrating on the material things of this world, citing that all things on earth can be destroyed or stolen (Mat. 6:19). Relative to an attempt to balance choices, much like balancing the scales by using a counterbalance, it is necessary for every child of the Creator, God, to recognize our place before Him. In the spiritual realm there is a need for undivided loyalty and love. God is our counterbalance. If we are not mindful of this, although we may inevitably experience comfort and security in exalting our circumstances and ourselves, and in denigrating others. To God we are an anathema; *deceitful and desperately wicked* (Jer. 17:9, KJV). We must remember that even as free men we are not our own. All children of God are to be servants of the Lord regardless of the cares of this world; and having liberty through Christ does not mean independence from God. It means experiencing a cherished relationship with Him which requires surrender of one's will. It does not mean doing whatever we want. At the cliff, there is much at stake relative in decision making. At the cliff one must find balance between the spiritual and the natural appetites. It is a moment in time to discover the true motivation of the heart. Our occasions on the cliff prove that decisions are based in this conflict between the spiritual and the natural; and when it becomes apparent that the conflict is more a matter of the self-will than the intellect, there can be a merger of reason with the heart.

Balancing the truths of God's Word amongst the many deceptions of Satan is conflict. The Word of God says the Believer is justified by faith apart from the law (Eph. 3:28). It says there is only one Lord, one faith and one baptism, and it says to love one another as we love ourselves (Eph. 4:5; John 13:34-35; 15:12, 17; Rom. 12:10; 13:8). Satan says, "I will give you this entire domain and its glory; for it has been handed over to me, and I give it to whomever I wish. Therefore if you worship before me, it shall all be yours" (Luke 4:6-8). Despite logical inclinations and the mundane aspects of this life, this life is transitory and uncertain, making it important to ensure that our existence is entrusted to God. Each Believer has been fashioned for the purposes of God, created for His family, instructed to become like Christ, modeled to serve Him, and made for His mission to commune with Him and make him known to others. Every human life has value. Scripture states that God "does not want anyone to perish but that all might have life abundantly" through Him (II Pet. 3:9; John 10:10). God has stated throughout the Bible that we are His children and spiritual heirs of His Divine nature, provision, protection, love and life at the moment we accept His gift of redemption "according to the riches of His grace" (Rom.8:29; Eph. 1:4-8). Conflict is evident in our families, circles of friends, community, under the watchful eye of an employer, schools, during the establishing of new churches, within religious centers, customary ministries and noted as doctrinal, cultural, ritual and philosophical differences as we seek to follow the leadings of God (Heb. 2:2-8; Jude 1). The Bible teaches that the knowledge and righteousness of humankind is nothing without the Holy Spirit and at a point in time, we will have to be willing to give up that which we consider ours, familiar and comfortable, for the promised reward that God has in store for us (I Peter 1). The deception that is debated by many is that our reward will be given predicated upon ascertainable actions or behaviors that we choose to display. Chapter 28 in the Book of Ezekiel informs us that Satan is successful at infusing a *me-first, self-willed* attitude among all humans except Jesus. According to God's plan every human creature has the opportunity in their lifetime to examine the uncommon gift of grace, to discern the availability of an uncommon life and to:

> Walk in a manner worthy of the Lord; pleasing Him in all respects, bearing fruit in every good work, increasing in the knowledge of God; and strengthened with all power, according to His glorious might, for the attaining of all steadfastness and patience; while joyously giving thanks to the Father, who has qualified us to share in the inheritance of the Saints in Light (Col. 1:10-12).

God does not want His children to develop close associations with the world because almost inevitably this leads to conflict with His standards. It jeopardizes the consistency of the Christian's witness for God because there is a spiritual force in the world that is at work to undermine the Christian (I Pet. 5:8). The cliffhanger experience is a demonstrably practical aspect of life which results in spiritual growth. Demonstrating to the watching world an active, intentional, purposeful faith is purposed by the cliffhanger. As we grow spiritually there are practical and observable behaviors. Throughout our mountain expedition we have the freedom to control our own behavior and must exercise this control responsibly. Along the journey of spiritual development the cliffhanger allows a choice between resistance and submission, the contrasts in conflict. James 4:7 states: "submit yourselves to God." Submission in the spiritual sense is representative of maturation. It is exhibited when you humble yourself before God, submerge yourself within Him, and learn to appreciate His perspectives and His conclusions (James 4:8-10). Spiritual maturity is submission to God's plan for His Kingdom. Resistance means the Believer has opposite interests and designs from God, making it impossible to be on any accord with Him. Accompanying resistance, there is dishonor to the Christian profession of faith through Jesus Christ leading to diminished loyalty, absence of service and rejection to the promptings of the Spirit of God. II Cor. 4:4 affirms that the resistant mind is blinded by Satan, producing conflict and creating incompatible allegiance. As the Spirit of God beckons, we undermine God's truth by placing faithfulness outside of Him. According to God's plan, as the Believer clings to the notion of God's preeminence and strives not to become unequally yoked or believe the lies of the unconverted; spiritual growth happens. Every Believer's experience at the crest of the mountain brings them towards a juncture of spiritual maturity. Despite the adversity prevalent with conflict, the cliffhanger is not a spiritual contest. It is a time to take a serious look at one's life, acknowledge the path chosen for you and "choose this day whom you will serve" to determine your purpose in this life and secure your eternal future (Josh. 24:15).

Have you ever noticed the terrain as you travel up mountains? The road appears as any other road. You hardly notice the assent except for the occasional view of the valleys and the accelerated roar of the car's engine. While travelling, there are various road signs that have been placed to dispel conflict. Traffic lights change color according to demand signaling stop, caution or go. Stop signs, yield signs and one-way signs all provide directives that, if ignored, may be punishable by law. Laws have been established as rules of engagement to help people identify wrongs, keep people safe and to maintain harmony. Have you witnessed the massive number of people who disobey traffic laws, thereby violating the rules of engagement? Just the other day, while traveling a two-lane stretch of the road, I encountered a sign which read, ONE LANE ROAD AHEAD. On the opposite side of the road, on the lane that cars travel a different direction, there was a larger sign which resembled a barricade to keep cars off the lane and it read, DO NOT ENTER; ROAD CLOSED indicating that there was only one lane available and I was driving on it. The lanes stretched about 500 feet from a stop sign to a traffic light at the main intersection. In order to continue on the road, reduced to a single lane by the signs, I had to wait at the stop sign until a few cars left the lane on which I was traveling. After a time of waiting, I was on my way. However, I had to stop several times along the way to allow clearance for the cars that were in my lane. Every time the other drivers came up to a large barricade sign they had to cross into my lane to get around it. I pondered, as I observed the many individuals who were totally disregarding the signs, disobeying the law, creating hazardous conditions and causing disharmony. Were the drivers being disobedient because they could see nothing which held them accountable? It has been documented that when people are granted the privilege of choice, the natural instinct is to give in to the carnal mind which is yielded to every vain and sensual desire and assuredly exalts personal values and morals. In reference to the narrative, the conflict occurs when the driver of one vehicle enters the lane of the driver going in the opposite direction. The car that controls the intersection has the right of way. Control generally means the car that is already into the intersection. If they arrive at the same time then the one to the right has the right-of- way or first in - first out. Of course all of these rules make an important assumption; the law assumes that both vehicles are obeying the other traffic laws such as speeding and following traffic signs. In this scenario, the posted road signs indicated; Do Not drive on the lane at all. This command was ignored by many. The overall behavior was "I am here now; had I known beforehand, I would have gone in another direction but now, to do the right thing would be an inconvenience for me. So I will just do the wrong thing and inconvenience someone else." To enforce the law and alleviate the challenge would require stationing a traffic cop along the barricaded road. This is how the Bible depicts humankind, always inclined to live outside of the will of God unless held to its standard of excellence by force. Historically, good, loving and positive relationships are not sustained by force.

The balanced perspective of choice is at the heart of Scripture and its Truth is absolute. The Bible reiterates this conflict as being *unequally yoked.* The origin of the phrase comes from having two oxen of unequal strength pulling a plow. The stronger one will dominate the other and the row of the plow will not be straight. The conflict of being unequally yoked exhibits compromised faith. It conjures an unfair burden or responsibility which may cause harm, discontent and misunderstandings; and conveys one not having equal strength, disposition or ability. Our narrative communicates this conflict as one of morality. For humanity, morality and "truth is what the majority thinks it is at a given moment, precisely because the majority is permitted to govern and redefine its values constantly."[16] Second Corinthians Chapter 6 verses 14-18 contrasts moral opposites inferring that wrong choices may compromise faith. The moral opposites contained in this Scripture are lawlessness versus righteousness, light versus darkness, Christ versus Belial and Believers versus unbelievers. Each contrast represents conflict that encompasses one's character, aptitude regarding the things of God, allegiance and faith. The effect of wrong choices can be burdensome directly and indirectly on all concerned. So the world is watching as the children of God decide, and care must be taken to avoid adherence to the principles of the world. The Book of Judges describes a time when *everyone did what was right in his own eyes* as one of the darkest periods of human history (Judg. 17:6;21:25). During this era the history of the children of God can be defined by four words: wrong-doing, repression, request and recovery. They began disregarding the Word of God then He allowed them to be enslaved by a neighboring nation. The people prayed to God for deliverance and He sent a judge to deliver them from their enemies. They would remain faithful to God only until the death of the judge. Then the cycle was repeated. The cliffhanger obliges that one make a final choice or judgment about their relationship with God but is not designed to increase spiritual maturity by force. It is a time for determining whether you will abide with Him without identifiable reinforcement, thereby developing a stronger bond with Him. It is a time to destroy deception, remove resistance, contain competition and select submission. Herein lies the *call to conflict.*

Open acknowledgment to live and preach the gospel of love and peace always arouses the attention of the evil one. Evil has to be subdued before peace can prevail. Therefore, while the eternal future that God proposes in Christ is comprised of peace and joy, the immediate result of his coming and of the delivery of the gospel message has been antagonism and bloodshed. We must remember that Jesus said: *I have not come to bring peace, but a sword.* The sword that Christ and his followers used in conflict is the Sword of the Spirit, but persecutors in every era have applied the carnal sword against Believers. This sword is raised because persecutors have as their assignment the destruction of the Kingdom of God and the elimination of its power. However, there is tremendous might manifested in the establishment of this Kingdom. Its fundamental strength is operational through love. When we consider that God's grace and love is given freely and is extended to all, this remarkable gift is to be affirmed as evidence of His Kingdom. As the Believer receives God's gifts of grace and love in the heart by the Holy Spirit, it is accepted by the mind and will; the very soul. Also, if these gifts are rejected, they are rejected at the depth of the soul. Correspondingly, the *call to conflict* is made apparent as these gifts once accepted or rejected assure the stability or disruption of our most significant relationships. Sometimes the call to conflict is a radical severing of social, marital, familial and business relationships. This presents the conflict represented by Jesus' question of, "who is my mother and brother?" saying that those who do the will of the Father are His family (Mat. 12:48, 50; Mark 3:33, 35). Frederick Douglass stated: "If there is no struggle, there is no progress. The struggle may be a moral one, a physical one or both but it must be a struggle. Power concedes nothing without demand. It never did and it never will."[17] Evil has its agenda and continually condemns the conscience, entangling the natural soul of man in unguarded moments at the cliff's edge. It seeks to affirm the concept of a Kingdom where there is love, liberty and no bias as contrary to reasonableness. Some people are conscientious relative to certain things but lack an overall conscience. To oppose Satan's evil schemes and to live morally upright, impartial and fair requires a conscience that has been enlightened by the Holy Spirit. As the Word of God states, some folk have their "conscience seared as with a hot iron" and its focus is selfish gain and pleasure (I Tim. 4:2). Individuals that are obedient and submit to doing the Father's will are often called to make hard choices during this life's journey (Matt. 25:20-23). Their perspective becomes aligned with the importance of fulfilling their purpose in God's plan and having the Kingdom of God in view enables them to approach the cliff's edge directly and without compromise. There is no neutral or lukewarm station which is acceptable to God (Rev. 3: 16). Each experience at the cliff should establish you closer to the realization that God's rule on earth is not to be thought of only as a future event. I have heard it said that people believe that we are in the land of the living going to a land of the dead. The Kingdom reality is that we are in the land of the dead *pressing toward* the land of the living (Phil. 3:7-16). The influence of His power and authority is manifest in the present. Of course this does not mean choosing is easy or made easier because we have been given faith and knowledge of the Kingdom. The institution of the Kingdom of God is a *call to conflict*. The conflict is exemplified as each person's difficulty embracing the virtues and perspectives of the King of Glory, while the king of darkness initiates doubt and confusion. The *call to conflict* is represented by the Sword, the Word of God, which reveals the war against humanity's endorsement of God's Kingdom that one chooses to either accept or reject. Faith and the acceptance of a divine reality will have its effect on our decisions and spiritual development up on the mountain peak.

The World is Watching

But brother goes to law with brother and that before unbelievers?
I Cor. 6:6

Every person is God's workmanship created for His purpose and designed to perform good works (Eph. 2:10). Each individual has been given a spirit at birth that empowers instinctually, making them a carnal human. Humankind has, what may be described as, an inborn pattern of behavior that is characteristic of its species and is often a response to specific environmental stimuli. Spirit is defined as the manifestation of expression exhibited by an individual. There are many explanations for spirit. Spirit is described as energy, enthusiasm, courage, personality and passion. It is a disposition of the mind and heart which can evolve and transcend, and impact the life of the person. Every person has received a spirit with the capacity to obtain knowledge of God, to develop relationship with Him, to be directed by His Holy Spirit and to become a righteous spiritual human. This is where the similarities between the carnal and the spiritual (Holy Spirit-led) human end. The Word of God contends that belief which descends to capture the heart, faith that transcends the rational mind, verbal confirmation and a renewed mentality by the Holy Spirit must take place for the carnal human's spirit to be transformed to the spiritual human (Rom. 10:9-10; 12:2-3). We are reminded of Nicodemus who was instructed by Jesus that a rebirth must occur to gain a righteous spirit; and Paul with his emphasis on becoming a new creation subsequent to the destruction of the old degenerate spirit (John 3:1-17; II Cor. 5:17).

As we take on this restored life in Christ to become a righteous spiritual human, the world is watching. Therefore, the Christian's spiritual experience is *a call to conflict.* The individual who has presented before God with contrition and repentance, who has accepted the Holy Spirit and who has been previously dead but made alive in Christ, perceives their God-created, breath-given life differently than persons who have not done this. An apocalyptic point on the mountain road is underway! Confronted with the difficulty of living a new life in Christ in an opposing world is a battle. The battle rages inside and outside as you grapple with choices. Various sins and weaknesses can make following the role of Jesus impossible. Then there are the subtleties of Satan that lead to discouragement, depression and disenfranchisement; and a world of people insisting that Christianity has no place in contemporary society. But, as Augustine, a historical, biblical scholar asserts, "there can be no *people,* but only a mob, where there is no *association* by a common sense of right; and no justice (that virtue which assigns to everyone his due)."[18] For the Believer, every mountain experience requires that you embark on a journey of recognizable conflict. Bounding off the mountain peak, you find yet another mountain must be climbed. Nevertheless, history reveals that with each cliff you conquer, spiritual knowledge, trust and wisdom are gained; and although the impending pinnacle is still quite difficult, you learn to let God guide and protect you. Not only is faith tested at the cliff; your identity is tested. Continual struggles with self, Satan and the world warrants the spiritual rest understood in the finished work of Christ. "So there remains a Sabbath rest for the people of God. Therefore let us be diligent to enter that rest, so that no one will fall, through *following* the example of disobedience" (Heb. 4:8-11). God provided redemption from sin and death for the entire world, both Jew and gentile, through the Messiah Jesus. As the redeemer and Helper of mankind, Jesus guided those who believed Him, claimed that "no one could come to the Father except through Him," and presented another Helper, the Holy Spirit, following His return to the Father (John 14:6; 16:7). The Believer is to rest in Christ as the Rescuer who has completed His task of delivering salvation and not try to work his way to God. The finished work of Christ alleviates merit and the obligation to share in God's plan to restore mankind's relationship with Him. It leaves no room for the Believer to boast of position before God. Humanity's fall from grace was by its own weakness while the sanctity of relationship in God is by His strength. Therefore, reconciliation is solely through the power and love of God. Paul wrote, "But by His doing you are in Christ Jesus, who became to us wisdom from God, and righteousness and sanctification, and redemption, so that, just as it is written: 'LET him who boasts, boast in the Lord." (1 Cor. 1:30-31). The world is watching the conflict between self-importance and the importance of surrendering to God.

Times on the mountaintop are moments that demand action. There comes a point in life when, as children of God, we ponder whether we contribute to the world and its disorderly state or participate with God in overcoming the world in preparation for His kingdom. As we contemplate our actions, we utilize our own sense of justice, what we consider normal and relevant; and our morals and fundamental beliefs. For Christians, actions regarding the disorderly state of the world and participation in overcoming the dismal state of a people living outside of the knowledge of God's grace often mean proselytizing and evangelizing. Proselytism is defined as the use of unfair and coercive methods or applying pressure to convince someone to leave one religion and join another; or exchange one state of spiritual existence for another. Evangelization is proclamation in word. It is an expressed witness of God as He is revealed through Jesus Christ in the Scriptures. Proclamation in word can be redefined by deeds with Jesus as our example. Jesus never forced His message or healing miracles on unbelievers. The crowds inquired or implored of Him. The commission to *go make disciples* includes the provision to proclaim where the Believer is accepted (Mat. 28:19-20; Mark 6:11). The majority of Jesus' healings were administered upon those who asked or sought remedy during assembly. A conflict emerges due in part to past experience, tradition and value teaching. Most religious practices, ideas and values are intricately bound in humanity's history. Jesus, teaching His disciples and the religious groups of His day emphasized that, being one with God, we should not stress one aspect of religious truth at the expense of another. In the Book of Matthew, Chapter 23, Jesus makes a concentrated attack on the religious authorities' disparity between the values of the Kingdom of God and their display of superficial religiosity (Mat. 5:17-48; 15:1-20). "The people of the covenant were unfaithful and yet faithful, in a strange way, to the absolute demands of the love of God."[19] The system of religious observance was being upheld, with an emphasis on adherence rather than the will of God and there was no reckoning of individual motives and performance. The "inclusivism of circumcision, Sabbath and sectarianism" enabled the preservation of their "religious and sociological identity" and their recognition as the chosen of God ushered in conceit. [20] Every individual is a product of a specifically tailored physical and spiritual environment. Everyone encounters conflict as belief systems are rebuked and questioned. *Paul, according to the wisdom given him, wrote there are some things that are hard to understand, which the ignorant and unstable twist to their own destruction* (II Pet. 3:15-16). The assertion is that Christians must be aware of this conflict and cautiously guard the spiritual component; to "live in holy conduct and godliness and take care that you are not carried away with the error of lawless people and lose your own stability" (II Pet. 3:11, 17). The Truths in God's Word reminds us that His Spirit gives us "power, love and a sound mind" (II Tim. 1:7). The cliffhanger is a time to discover the depth of our understanding. It also reminds us of the need to take action, stand strong and determined in what we believe.

The world is watching, so be steadfast, immovable, always abounding in the work of the Lord (I Cor. 15:58). This aspect of your journey cannot be simply relegated to private emotions and personal inhibitions or it would appear that Christianity is meaningless and the promises of God and His Kingdom void. The Kingdom of God is the subject of the Bible with an emphasis on "overcoming the restrictions of peculiarity" offered to the elect of the Old Covenant and "seeking to embrace all races of men," ushered in by the New Covenant, thus the rebirth of the elect as the body of Christ.[21] The maturation of one's identity as a Christian often incites a consuming and even frantic attempt to fulfill the commission of God. As we study God's Word, we discover that the Lord requires Believers to develop a personal intimacy with Him through the Holy Spirit. As this intimacy matures it becomes inclusive of others. One does not travel these mountains in a vacuum. As it is written: how can you love a God that you have not seen and hate your brother whom you see? (I John 4:20). The Bible is replete with sanctions to care for the poor in body, soul and spirit; to look after the sick, elderly, widow and disabled and to demonstrate love for God's people. Oftentimes, we can choose to care for the former but love for our brothers and sisters may be absent. The conflict within this period of decision is that we must surmise the Truth based upon both the teachings of the Word of God and from discovery compiled through living. The experience of discovery through living interestingly fashions our behaviors for good or for bad. Many of our relationships are modeled based upon positive and negative experiential exposure and how it is processed. What this means is, we tend to base our associations and decisions on those we witness. Researchers believe that children who grow up in homes where there is unfaithfulness to the marital partner tend to view infidelity as normal. This is because parents are a child's ultimate source of acquired knowledge and learning therefore, when a parent strays, the children assent to this type of behavior. Correspondingly, these children tend to be the benefactor of unfaithful relationships or to be the recipient of the cheating when they are in relationships. It hurts them and can often lead children to pattern their lives and the way they interact with their partners after the example parents have set. Parents don't often truly understand or realize the extent that their actions will harm the children. Many times for Believers, the decision on the mountain cliff is deliberate defiance against known principles and values such as priority consideration of others (Phil. 2:3). There is expectation of approval for these behaviors, somehow justified by some personal standard of righteousness in lieu of the Truths in God's Word. Often untoward behaviors are dismissed as inconsequentially due to laziness on our part when it is apparently governed by indifference, selfishness and unconcern. We retort, much like Cain regarding Abel, "Am I my brother's keeper?" Religious piety abounds yet, Jesus reproved expressed religious piety as hypocrisy (Mat. 23: 13-15). Still, the world is watching as complacency and individual achievement give sway to division and persecution from generation to generation; and Kingdom building seems of no importance. This, not only affects the Believer's individual spiritual growth, it impacts a nation.

In the midst of disharmony, Christianity is confronted on all levels to defend against the various worldviews like evolution, same sex marriage and adultery. The assertion of many in the world is that Christians should be grateful to attend a church of choice, pay no church taxes; that they are allowed proclamations of faith in public forums, to display Christian icons on owned property, permitted missionary visits and to publish Christian literature. The Bible discloses that children of God are only visitors having a temporary stay on earth (Ps.39:12). With current philosophy attempting to discredit Christianity, the visitor image is a more marked reality as the Christian religion becomes distinguished as a wanderer with no residence. The ranking of Christianity on this earth is similar to the status of an alien sojourner. Anti-religion or atheism is prevailing and may be identified as a form of religion much like nondenominational places of worship become denominations. An allegation is that Christianity as a system of belief is under attack. In reality the very existence of a Sovereign God in the conscience of mankind is under attack. Every remark of persecution is more than a simple expression against religious principles and practices. They are expressions that the very core of a moralistic humane society is being destroyed. The world's argument is about choice and rights when it offers no choice or rights for Christianity. This is why children of God are exhorted as workmen to *study the Word of Truth* so that one is able to *rightly* divide it making approval by God apparent that there be no need for disgrace (II Tim. 2:15, KJ V). Modern Scholars typically translate the meaning and usage of this English word *study* as "hit the books, learn, analyze, investigate, examine, scrutinize, be diligent, work hard, do your best, or earnestly contemplate." But the Greek word literally means make speed or hurry. It conveys the sense of making earnest effort or be prompt to labor. Therefore, to rightly divide the Word and to show ourselves approved by God; God's charge is, "Hurry to do it! Be quick about it! Be diligent at it. Do your best; and make the truth plain." We are mandated by our actions and behaviors "to proclaim the Lord's death until He comes" (I cor. 11:26). We are to break bread in remembrance of Jesus' death and to drink from the cup in remembrance of the new covenant which was ratified by the blood of Jesus (Mat. 26:26-29) "Our exhortation did not come from deceit or uncleanness, nor was it in guile. But as we have been approved by God; entrusted with the gospel, even so we speak, not as pleasing men, but *pleasing* God who tests our hearts" (I Thess. 2:3). The unjust world, where the natural inclination is toward evil thoughts, murders, adulteries, fornications, thefts, false witness and blasphemies, needs a demonstration of the Truths found in the message of the Bible because if God does not rule, these general characteristics of humanity abound (Mat. 15:19). Disciples of Christ are chosen to advocate for God to the world in word and deed, by the acceptable behaviors and attitudes inevitable of that harmonious Kingdom. Paul reminds the reader that despite worldly efforts which seek the demise of the Gospel we must withstand the conflict:

> Therefore, since we have this ministry, as we received mercy, we do not lose heart, but we have renounced the things hidden because of shame, not walking in craftiness or adulterating the Word of God, but by the manifestation of truth commending ourselves to every man's conscience in the sight of God. And even if our gospel is veiled, it is veiled to those who are perishing, in whose case the god of this world has blinded the minds of the unbelieving so that they might not see the light of the gospel of the glory of Christ, who is the image of God. For we do not preach ourselves but Christ Jesus as Lord, and ourselves as your bond-servants for Jesus' sake. For God, who said, "Light shall shine out of darkness," is the One who has shone in our hearts to give the Light of the knowledge of the glory of God in the face of Christ. But we have this treasure in earthen vessels, so that the surpassing greatness

> of the power will be of God and not from ourselves; we *are* afflicted in every way, but not crushed; perplexed, but not despairing; persecuted, but not forsaken; struck down, but not destroyed; always carrying about in the body the dying of Jesus, so that the life of Jesus also may be manifested in our body. For we who live are constantly being delivered over to death for Jesus' sake, so that the life of Jesus also may be manifested in our mortal flesh. (II Cor. 4:1-11)

The truth is, unless the carnal spirit of a person is exchanged for the Holy Spirit by faith in Jesus Christ through the teachings of the Bible, it is all implausible and Christianity will remain in conflict. Standing at the edge looking over into the abyss brings the realization that belief in God and faith through Christ cannot be limited to become a self-centered, self-seeking, or self-directed component of our lives. There, at the edge, we are compelled to see the need for an ultimate solution and the World is watching. *Therefore let us draw near with confidence to the throne of grace, so that we may receive mercy and find grace to help in time of need* (Heb. 4:16). As we walk along the mountain peak, the cliffhanger is a *call to conflict* where delay and wavering causes divergence and complacence; and where contrasting worldviews have a deleterious effect on spiritual development.

The Book of Genesis chapter 22 provides an account, for a watching audience, of the relationship between Abraham and God. In it there is a portrayal that the cliffhanger is a call to conflict. It is the depiction of Abraham offering his son, Isaac as a sacrifice. "The God of glory appeared to Abraham and said to Him *depart from your country and your relatives and come into the land that I will show you*" (Acts 7:2-3). Abraham, not knowing where he was going at his initial call was not hesitant to follow God, but this was only the beginning of his cliff hanger experience. He had many tests, each culminated in the receipt of God's promise. Abraham's most notable stand at the cliff was to sacrifice Isaac. The Bible says that Abraham, so full of faith in anticipation of his day on the cliff, rose up early (Gen. 22:1-12). Making preparations for the sacrifice he saddled his donkey, cut and gathered wood for fire and a knife; and set out for the place God instructed which was approximately a three days journey. On the way, there was much time to think about this trial. Abraham's worldview was based on foreknowledge and relationship. God had always kept His promises. However, Abraham was still only human, with limited understanding and with natural concerns for the tangible. His tests determined his capacity to trust God even when it appeared absurd to the natural mind. As he climbed the mountain he considered many things. What would God do? How would He do it? When would it occur? Once realizing that Isaac would be the likely sacrifice he pondered: How could Isaac die when God made the promise of many descendants? How will God fulfill His promise now that Isaac's life was at stake? Why did God choose to jeopardize Isaac's life? Abraham was being asked to give up Isaac. What an extraordinary request, how can this be Abraham's assignment? This was the supreme test of his faith and Abraham surrendered. He completely succumbed to the Holy Spirit of God. In the story, there was no exhibition of the carnal nature. There was no voice of protest raised. He acquiesced fully. Abraham took the enormous step from the cliff, much like Jesus, obeying God despite the consequences and to benefit all of God's children. The Word of God affirms that the Gospel was preached to Abraham in his day, for God had allowed him to foresee that He would justify the Gentiles by faith, seeing that in Abraham, *all nations shall be blessed* (Gal.3:8). Even Jesus said, "*Your father Abraham rejoiced to see my day; he saw it and was glad*" (John 8:56).

> In hope against hope he believed, so that he might become a father of many nations according to that which had been spoken, SO SHALL YOUR DESCENDANTS BE. Without becoming weak in faith he contemplated his own body, now as good as dead since he was about a hundred years old, and the deadness of Sarah's womb; yet, with respect to the promise of God, he did not waver in unbelief but grew strong in faith, giving glory to God, and being fully assured that what God had promised, He was able also to perform. Rom. 4:18-21

Abraham's willingness to obey God regardless of the outcome emphasized his faith. His faith was credited to him as righteousness (Gen. 15:6). Abraham was justified by a faith that becomes evident before men through works (Rom. 4:1-3; James 2:21). It is true, blessed and humbling that Jesus the Christ died for the sins of the world, but He first died, lest we forget, for God. The spiritual history of Abraham was marked by many mountain peak decisions which involved conflict. He was called away from his native land and kindred, he had to allow his nephew Lot to choose his way and be separated from him, he had to believe and conquer doubt that a child would be born to him and his wife Sarah and finally, he was instructed to offer up Isaac as a human sacrifice (Gen.12:1; 13:1-18; 22:2). People are reflections of culture and surroundings. Abraham functioned counter to his cultural environment trusting in God. The cliff is a fact of our mountain travels. Each traverse of the mountain and every cliff encountered are logged as a past experience at the next occasion. Since the cliff is about transformation, how we are changed by our past experiences elicit an eventual altered response to our new experience. As the world looks on the journey of life for all of God's children is a series of mountain cliffs and it is during these circumstances that Christian character can be developed. The story of Abraham's life is an example that all Believers will be tested many times. God's demand is, "give Me thine heart (Prov. 23:26, KJV). He does not demand our intellect, talents or money. He desires the heart with its cares and passions. As Scripture states, where your treasure is, there your heart will be, also" (Luke 12:34). God requires "truth in the inward parts; for the mouth speaks that which fills the heart" (Psalm 51:6; Luke 6:45). There were two witnesses who observed Abraham and Isaac go up on the mountain to worship without the normal sacrifice and then return without incident to be *greatly blessed* (Gen. 22:17). During his cliffhanger experiences, which were besieged by conflict, Abraham embraced his faith to transfigure his understanding, increase his spiritual maturity and earned him right standing with God in the eyes of men.

Unequally Yoked

> *Beloved, do not believe every spirit, but test the spirits to see whether they are from God; because many false prophets have gone out into the world.*
>
> I John 4:1

The cliffhanger as a call to conflict is distinguished during relationship decisions. These choices are based upon ideologies, emotions, spiritual and psychological needs. Many close associations almost inevitably lead to compromise and intertwining lives suggests a commonality inclusive of tradition, era, culture and genealogy but, often is not enslaved by it. A collision occurs when you come into conflict with someone or something. A collision of worlds occurs between the natural and the supernatural, between the concepts of bondage and freedom, when conventional meets contemporary and exceptional meets customary. Above the chasm between them, attraction urges; instigating a collision. These encounters can be violent or subtle, each having a direct impact with obvious incompatibility. Expectations can collide, ideas clash, realities seem awry and radical views conflict. The beguiling nature of such encounters imposes significant uncertainty. Paul wrote urging children of God not to become entangled with individuals that do not believe the Word of God (II Cor. 6:14). God prohibits His children to engage in close associations with people who undermine biblical values. The encounter incites challenge and challenge may cause yielding. When the Believer compromises the standards of God they jeopardize the consistency of the Christian witness for Him. It is written that children of God are to be a sanctified people yet, looking around we often find that the opposite is true. Many attempt to fit in by making the decision to live as unbelievers or feel disconcerted, disconnected and are not sure why. This is disquieting as it presents many limitations along the mountain journey. We must expect many alterations in the condition and circumstances of any relationship. All relationships of choice should be governed by prudence. A plan or course of action intended to influence and determine decisions, actions, and other matters. Prudence, though often synonymous with cautious, must not be regulated to fear of taking risk. The prudence of which the Bible speaks is often associated with wisdom, insight, and knowledge and is the ability to judge with regard to appropriate actions at a given time and place. Proverbs 8:12 states: "I, wisdom, dwell with prudence, and I find knowledge *and* discretion." All choices should be regulated by prudence as it often produces integrity. Integrity means being the kind of person God intended when he designed you. The evidence of integrity lies in one's temperament and behaviors established as acceptable for children of God. Someone who is honest, reliable, and recognizably one with God through intimate knowledge of Him, opposing the natural contemptuous nature. Knowledge of the Lord is effective to eradicate the natural affinity for the wicked and profane. It is also necessary to establish behaviors that are not infuriating and dangerous. This knowledge is attained through study of God's Word, fellowship with God, His family and prayer. For the child of God, this life is not being lived to reinforce one's own agenda or to carry out one's own ideas, which is the natural tendency, but God's. As the Apostle Paul wrote: "For the good that I want, I do not do, but I practice the very evil that I do not want" (Rom. 7:19). Herein lies the conflict. We are called to leave behind all influences that keep us from being the person God has planned for us to be. In consideration of the conflict, Christians must concur to a specified relationship with God as His sons and daughters, otherwise no relationship exists and holding certain dissimilar perspectives and attempting to intertwine them is akin to the absurdity of joining righteousness with unrighteousness or mingling light with darkness. The mountaintop is a place which determines commitment; whether we will debase and degrade ourselves or stand true to the commands and cause of Christ.

The Bible explains that God made human beings in His image while knowing that we would sin. The conflict in the relationship between an omnipotent, omnipresent, all-wise God and mankind is the personal decision of a loving Creator that allows choice. Most people cannot fathom the possibility of such intimacy. The familiarity requisitioned by the Word of God is a matter of vulnerability through faith which is impossible for the human spirit. Ultimately, our downfall originates with our own wills and desires. "All that is in the world, the lust of the flesh and the lust of the eyes and the boastful pride of life, is not from the Father, but is from the world" (I John 2: 16). Those who delight in the power and might of their own humanity and exalt themselves as gods have the propensity for unrighteousness and evil (Mat. 15:19). The Bible says their aspiration is physical pleasure (Eph. 2:3). Every person is awakened each day to the sins of this world. For many, there is something within that says this world cannot be all that there is, even though this is the only world that we have ever known. Even the ancient prophets, who foretold of the Savior to come as the truth of God's grace, were met with opposition. As it is written: "They come to you as people come, and sit before you *as* My people and hear your words, but they do not do them, for they do the lustful desires *expressed* by their mouth, *and* their heart goes after their gain" (Ezek. 33:31). The corruption, the lies, and the pretense have always been around causing insecurity, frequently leading to feelings of isolation, sadness and feeling unloved. The rational mind does not quite comprehend, but even the rational mind knows that the idea of sin is contrary to godliness and the spiritual being that God has created. Since individuals are the product of environmental exposure many discover that although a child of the Promise, a child chosen for God's purposes before the physical world began and being unaware of their status as heir to The King to receive an eternal inheritance, we become unequally yoked with the prince of darkness who has us in bondage. The revelation of this comes through an unyielding search of Scriptures, prayer and supplication. The Bible proclaims that all of humankind is engaged in a spiritual battle where good and evil spirits vie for the soul (Eph. 6:10-20). Once the two worlds have been disclosed in the spirit and to the conscience mind, the two worlds collide and a decision has to be made to choose between them. This is a cliff hanger experience which may or may not lead to relationship with the God of the universe. "As God has said, be not unequally yoked; I will be your God and you shall be my people, I will be a Father unto you, and you shall be my sons and daughters" (II Cor. 6: 14, 18). Sometimes this moment on the cliff is a conscious event. For many it happens within the subconscious. At the edge of your cliff, you are being alerted to the battle for your soul and you have to choose sides. If you are able to discern this, then you will become more aware that the decisions made during this time will have an everlasting impact and affect your spiritual maturity. If you are not able to discern the matter, then you are destined to repeat the thing until you do.

Dissension occurs between the concepts of bondage and freedom. Bondage is characterized by the Mosaic Law as the representative of man's sin. Freedom is characterized by grace as the representative gift of God through Jesus Christ. It is widely accepted that the Scriptural passage, II Corinthians 6:14: "be not unequally yoked together with unbelievers" references that Christians are not to marry those who do not believe the message of the Gospels. This is true, but limiting and relegates this message from the Word of God to the physical, natural realm. The Bible provides deeper insight regarding application of this familiar passage addressing concepts of bondage and freedom. Significant to the New Testament is the admonition not to abandon the freedom offered by the love of God in Jesus. Understanding the acquired freedom in Christ enables one to observe the ensuing bondage that prevails in laws and traditions. Individuals become assailed by depression, disillusionment and despair when required to strive for their own righteousness. Conversely, being justified by faith alone brings peace and allows the Believer to pursue the will of God and to *walk by faith* (II Cor. 5:7). The yoke of bondage oppresses, condemns and accuses. It is imposed by self-righteousness or by an individual's self-condemnation. The foregone conclusion is a discordant relationship with God; and a collision of worlds between justification by the law and justification by grace. The presumption is, since Jesus was sacrificed according to the plan of God to fulfill the requirements of the law, and yet Believers function as if still under the binding agreement of the law, then the gospel is not believed as it is written. Accordingly, anyone imposing this yoke of bondage may be construed as unbelievers or most commonly identified in Scripture as false teachers. Manner of worship should not be determined as lawlessness and choice should not create litigation. Jesus renounced outward displays of piety, impropriety and reputation during discourse with the religious sects of His day. Contrary to popular opinion, behaving well, baptism, partaking of the sacraments, fancy attire and church membership does not matter much in the accomplishment of salvation. The Book of Hebrews, Contemporary English Version, chapter 10 verses 28 and 29 states: "If accused of breaking the Mosaic Law, that person could be put to death. But it is much worse to dishonor God's Son, disgrace the blood of the promise and insult the Holy Spirit, who shows us mercy." Dispute over religiosity, the inherent conflict within the body of Christ, compounds contention which is in opposition to the love that God intends among His children. The conflict evident by the notion of bondage and free incites the question: A*re we crucifying Jesus again?* "How severe should the punishment be for the one who has trampled underfoot the Son of God, and has regarded as unclean the blood of the covenant by which he was sanctified, and has insulted the Spirit of grace" (Heb.10:29)? The discord in the Body of Christ is indistinguishable from the worldliness spoken of by Paul whose urging to keep oneself free from idolatry, come out from the midst of the unclean and be separate from the unrepentant, is to protect the Believer from defiling both body and spirit (II Cor. 6:11-18: 7:1). This is a cliff on which many still remain.

You have a coworker who professes to be a Christian but, from your perspective, is not God-fearing and their ungodliness is demonstrated by the words of his mouth. "Can both fresh water and salt water flow from the same spring" (James 3:11, NIV)? You have never heard anyone curse and swear so much. You become cynical and more skeptical of your Christian friend's preaching about being a disciple of Christ and being changed by God's Spirit but, something inside has been pressuring you to change. In spite of life's normal difficulties, you have been fine. But lately, you have been thinking about going to church on Sundays. You never went as a child. Only one of your friends attends church regularly and you have discounted him as just being different. One day, you decide to accept a friend's invitation to a program at the church. While there the choir sings a beautiful song led by someone very familiar. You realize it is your coworker. Immediately your spirit is vexed because of the history you two share. Your coworker is singing to God while behaving unlike any way you imagine a Christian should behave when at work and from your finite perspective living a lie. Your mountain journey has brought you to this time and place. At the crest of the mountain you ponder your situation. Should you talk this over with the friend who invited you to church? The actions of your coworker should not have any effect on your choices, should they? Your coworker's morality or immorality has nothing to do with you, Right? Should a Christian's conduct be different than a non-Christian's conduct? After all they are just people. Should conduct be similar between Christians? You have heard that the Bible says *do not be unequally yoked together*, can this refer to the differences between professing Christians? It is confusing for you. Why you are even thinking about this is amazing. It is not something you ever believed, anyway. Spiritual growth is evident as you realize, standing there at the edge of the cliff, that in the moment of decision you must be true in your convictions, increase your knowledge and become more spiritually astute. It is mystifying to have innate notions of uniqueness and then realize something must be done to be freed from the sense of imprisonment in the wake of such controversy. It is no longer your coworker's issue. What you perceive as Christian behavior without benefit of routine fellowship and teaching brings the situation back to you. You begin to realize that you have been bound and it is time for you to understand the message of the Bible to make more accurate observations. Standing at the cliff you are acutely aware of the band of evil surrounding you, attempting to keep you from your destiny. Its efforts are to harness the power within you and to keep you utterly distracted so that your focus is on your coworker rather than on the God of the Bible. If you give in, you will have succumbed to fear, disappointment, insecurity and insufficiency. So, to escape this bondage of entrapment you must choose the freedom God offers and step off of the cliff believing "in Him all things hold together" (Co. 1:17).

When exceptional and customary worlds collide it conjures a divisive paradigm. Customary is synonymous with conventional meaning, what has always been. Customary takes into account what is done in practice and what is expected in behavior. It implicates habitual, routine and established customs rather than principles, precepts and laws. Customary is indicative of the call and response or action-reaction methodology. On the other hand, exceptional means nonconforming to the general pattern of behaviors and practices. It comprises the unusual and uncommon that can stir emotions, incite differences and exhibit qualities and abilities exceedingly above expectations. The command to not be unequally yoked to unbelievers is disconcerting to some because it means that it is mandatory to be exceptional. Moses' world was exceptional. He sought God after he was summoned by Him. He entreated God for answers and received them. Alternatively, the Israelites' world was customary. They were fearful and lacked confidence in establishing a relationship with God, although every generation received evidence that relationship is what God required. They chose to maintain the status quo; the tried and true, by having Moses whom they perceived as someone closer to God speak for them. It behooves everyone to realize that the dilemma of the cliffhanger has always been a choice to trust God, take Him at His Word and abide with Him; a choice between customary and exceptional. This truth brings enlightenment while standing at the cliff's edge where spirit building is paramount. However, the contrast between exceptional and customary relative to spiritual things is hard to comprehend. It would appear the errors of the ages are destined to be repeated again and again. Exceptional seeks the more excellent way of love by refusing to rest on its laurels and the accepted norms, searching the Scriptures under the guidance of God's Spirit and discerning His Truths. Jesus and His apostles exemplified the exceptional. Under-supplied by the world's standards and reliant on the generosity of humanity, they had no gold or silver, and spoke of no houses or lands; still they possessed the treasures of heaven. They were ridiculed, chastised, surrendered under the lash of the law, imprisoned and killed, but remained true to their task. Desirous to promote the spiritual welfare of all to whom they preached, they sought mutual affection as all who believe are heirs of the Kingdom. An exceptional world enables partnership and being in agreement with or on one accord assures the ethical demands of the relationship in the form of fruit that is "good, right and true" (Eph. 5:9). Contrasting the customary world, common partnering where no advancement is derived from the venture is like the fig tree that did not bear fruit. It is good-for-nothing. Customarily, the temple was a physical structure where God made His presence known to Israel, now, exceptionally, through Christ, the temple has been transformed and God's temple became the people themselves (II Cor. 6:6). Therefore, do not be unequally yoked. This indicates that every child of God is exclusively His and must forsake all associations that are incompatible with the loyalty incumbent upon His ownership. The hierarchical, authoritarian arrangement of the established religious order, then and now, that produces a lack of comfortable communion due to a haughty philosophy is customarily an expression of misplaced and incompatible loyalties. Even more amazing is the necessity to aspire to be exceptional without reward. The customary world stance is, if I do a particular thing, I will be rewarded. So for example: if I accept God's gift of redemption, I will be restored to Him. If I accept Jesus Christ's sacrificial death, I will be forgiven and if I confess the Lord and His resurrection, I will have eternal life and the Bible proposes rewards as crowns for works, although it mandates that attaining crowns cannot be the motive for works. The exceptional, uncommon world, agrees that the customary stance has merit, however, insightfully recognizes that "every good and perfect gift comes from God," is initiated by God and conceived in Him (James 1:17). Therefore, the only reward that matters is God. "Whatever is bound on earth shall be bound in heaven and whatever is loosed on earth shall be loosed in heaven" and our mind should be set on this groundwork for eternity (Mat. 16:19).

Unbelievers say there is no God; that belief in God is unnatural and irrational. The argument for God is faith, not rationality. It is choosing to believe. Having the opportunity to believe, the unbeliever choosing to reject God is equivalent to being against Him. The Word of God affirms that "because they did not receive the love of the truth so as to be saved, God will send upon them a deluding influence so that they will believe what is false in order that they all may be judged who did not believe the truth" (II Thess. 2:11-12). How frightening. According to Charles Spurgeon, "faith in God becomes the crown of all belief; the most assured of all confidences."[22] Most doubters believe that the idea of an all-encompassing God poses a contradiction. With the customary argument in view, relationship with God is conceived as adopting a religion's way of life. The contemporary perspective of faith is a "purely natural exercise, which consists of an opinion held in good faith without necessary reference to proof."[23] From the exceptional perspective, faith is characterized by a passionate spiritual loyalty to God often exhibited by a high standard of obedience to godly principles and a God-centered, purposeful existence. Personal commitment is inherent in faith. Faith is intelligible; demanding a willingness to venture beyond the parameters of philosophical reason. It is knowing against understanding; being unaware of what lies beyond the limits of speculative thought. We "believe more instead of less; believe more in the pardon of sin, more in the renovation by the Holy Spirit, more in the everlasting covenant, more in the love that had no beginning and will never cease."[24] At the edge of the mountain, choosing entails risk, but one cannot avoid or reduce risk by refusing to choose. Although everyone's spiritual maturity is individual, ultimately, for everyone, one's passions shape decision. Avoidance is as risky as faithful obedience. We are directed by God to take risks. Risk is demonstrated as 'trust in God rather than any presumed action by Him," for example, "the object of Abraham's faith was not God's promise, his faith rested on God Himself."[25] Through the admonition of Paul, God demands that we choose sides: "Do not be bound together with unbelievers" (I Cor. 6:14). Moved by faith to assent to Christianity is a miracle whereby the exceptional challenges all the principles of understanding that lead one to believe and to do what is contrary to custom and experience.

A final collision of worlds occurs when conventional meets contemporary. Convention is identified by tradition; what has always been done. While contemporary is concerned with modern; the new thing that is currently being done. Traditionally, within monotheistic (one God only) religions, the foundational structure of society has been dominated by males. Scripture portrays ancient civilization as husbands rule over wife, fathers rule over children, masters rule over slave and in literature leaders were males because this distinction had cultural relevancy to the people. For many years most societies were hierarchical. Even women of great financial wealth and stature had to pretend to be men or conceal their identity as an official ruler. (i.e. China's Empress Dowager Cixi or George Eliot the pen name of Marian Evans) Women soldiers of the Civil War disguised themselves as men, assumed masculine names and managed to hide the fact that they were female while they lived in camp, suffered in prisons and died for their respective causes. All things were centered on the male and were most beneficial to him. In the midst of this patriarchal egotistical world there is conflict between the natural world and the spiritual world. The Word of God proclaims that "there is neither Jew nor Gentile, neither slave nor free, nor is there male and female, for you are all one in Christ Jesus" (Gal. 3:28). The narrative of Rahab affirms that women are central to God's reign and purposes. Moreover, Rahab was not only female she was a Gentile and a prostitute. She is presented as very unconventional in a land ruled by convention, yet God used her mightily. She lived, geographically and morally, on the edge of society. Her house was located in the wall of the city. Two spies went into the city of Jericho and entered the house of Rahab. Everyone in the city had heard of the God of Israel and when confronted with the needs of the two spies, Rahab went into action due to her respect and fear of their God. She offered protection as a hiding place for the spies who were in danger from the authorities and she faced the risk of being killed if caught. Perhaps the reports that had been circulating regarding the Israelites and their God would save her and her family. Should she ask these men? She had never been able to trust strange men before; could she put her trust in these men? She did not intend to perish at the hands of the Israelites with the rest of Jericho. She knew that if she did nothing it would be to her peril and all of her family. So she made a conscious decision to act in faith based on what she had heard about God who had dried up the water of the Red Sea allowing the Israelites passage from Egypt; "for the Lord God is God, in heaven above and on the earth below" (Josh. 2:10-14). Sincere faith means no one can serve two masters (Mat. 6:24). This affirms the impossibility of maintaining an unequal yoke. Rahab decided that she would go the way of the Israelites instead of the way of the Gentiles because the Lord had made known to her that He had already given them the land of Jericho. After the Israelites conquered Jericho, Rahab and her family was spared as promised. She lived amongst the Jewish nation and grew in grace and spiritual maturity. She later became the wife of Salmon, and the mother of Boaz. Notice that the contemporary conflicts with convention. In a culture that subordinates woman, Matthew lists Rahab among five other women in his genealogy of Jesus; Rahab's faith brought her into an immeasurable inheritance. She went from a Gentile prostitute to the lineage of Jesus Christ and "by faith the harlot Rahab did not perish with those who did not believe" (Heb.11:31). She refused to be unequally yoked together with convention and her familiar community; instead she chose to follow a different path and by faith stepped off the cliff. Her spiritual development was demonstrated as she ignored the conflict between the natural and the supernatural, convention and contemporary; exceptional and customary; and bondage and free.

The Lies We Believe

I am amazed that you are so quickly deserting Him who called you by the grace of Christ, for a different gospel.

Gal. 1:6

Conflict for the Believer is often displayed as divergent perspectives. Christians are instructed by the Word of God not to judge the motives, appearance, service or conscience of other Believers (Rom. 14:1-5). However, the natural inclination is to *size up* and formulate opinions about others. In the Book of Matthew, chapter 6 versus 19-24, Jesus teaches His followers that their thoughts and intentions should be centered on an eternal future. Each disciple of Christ is to be guided by spiritual insight. Spiritual insight is the supernatural ability to discern spiritual things. It is the ability to perceive God's standard of right. It is the capacity to discern whether thoughts, actions and attitudes are conformed to the likeness and teachings of Jesus; "to destroy arguments and every lofty opinion raised against the knowledge of God, and take every thought captive to obey Christ" (II Cor. 2:5). Jesus describes the natural eye of the physical body as one which imparts light and illuminates the mind, enabling sight. He contends that the eyes effect vision and bad eyes impair visibility making what might be identified as light determined to be darkness. It is necessary from a spiritual perspective that the collective body of Christ comprehends this concept. The analogy of the good and bad eyes signifies divergent perspectives which affect what we believe. Good eyes belong to individuals, whose motives are unpolluted by the ideologies of the world, singly guided by God's purposes and centered on an eternal future. The bad eye is obscured, often having double-vision as the Believer attempts to exist in both the natural and the spiritual worlds. Arrogance, conceit, greed, covetousness and envy are the sustenance for the lies that are believed when spiritual vision is lost. The Book of Jude is a letter to Christians who were being led astray by teachers they thought were legitimately righteous but were false teachers. He reminds them of the gifts of faith and knowledge they themselves had received and urged that they fight for the Truth. Lies present rival claims to the truths of God's Word and we must choose between them. We become spiritually blind "exchanging the truth of God for a lie worshipping the *created* rather than the Creator" (Rom. 1: 25). The lies we believe can cause the Believer to display a lack of hospitality due to pride or envy and a lack of support for a co-laborer and traveling companion while not discerning the counterfeit principles that are surmised from conflicting points of view (III John). People believe the lies of Satan now as they did at creation. Individuals seeing God's mighty works in their lives attribute the visible results to their own abilities, strength or luck. Many do not understand or do not want to understand the concept that every human being is sinful from birth. They ask, how can an innocent child be delivered into this world a sinner? The acceptance of Satan from the beginning of mankind's existence enables the demonic spirit to exert his power at the moment of the first breath. However, *God provides a way of escape* along with the power to choose (I Cor. 10:13).

The Book of Genesis in the Bible answers questions about the origins of the universe, mankind, the varied life forms; and sin and evil in the world. It conveys the early history details of man and of God's chosen people. It informs that every human is superbly designed by a highly intelligent Creator, on the basis of His decision, for His purpose and not by chance. The Bible states that God made both male and female in His image. Mankind, as the creature, has the freedom to choose, the ability to distinguish between good and evil and the capacity to relate to the Creator. Human beings, the only creation designed in the image of the Creator, are being opposed internally and externally for this identity. The Bible asserts that Satan is the ruler of this world and uses the people who do not accept God in his attack. To address the point which the world and the devil are attacking Christians, let us consider the events immediately following the creation and fall of man. From the beginning of creation God made humanity male and female. The value of gender and roles was established in the beginning. The male's directive to manage with the female to be his help is of inestimable worth in the world God has provided. At first glance the roles are described as caretaker and companion. The foundation of marriage was instituted for propagation and to illustrate the characteristic of God; His love (Gen. 2:24; Eph. 5:25-29). The two shall become one flesh. Consequently they are no longer two spirits, but one in spirit. And the Word says, *what God has joined together, let no man separate* (Mark 10: 6-9). The capacity to become one is necessary because of the distinct and complimentary differences between them. As two halves make a whole, the male and the female comprise the consolidated intimacy promoted by the Creator and God established gender differences to enable a divinely inspired society. Following the creation of man

(Adam), God gave instructions in reference to specific responsibilities for the man. After, the woman was created as a suitable helper for him. The order of creation and the initial directives given to Adam indicates a unique leadership and headship role for him. Adam was a perfect, sinless man and Eve was a perfect, sinless woman. Both were in relationship with God, who had given them the aptitude for acts of volition. "God blessed them; and God said to them, "Be fruitful and multiply, and fill the earth, and subdue it; and rule over the fish of the sea and over the birds of the sky and over every living thing that moves on the earth" (Gen 1:28).

After the fall, God established a covenant with them, in Jesus, and with all of humanity. This covenant proposes the condition that each distinctly human creature, must be born again to be God's representative on earth and although given the ability to choose, must be, governed by God's Spirit. Until then, as presented in the Bible, all of mankind, both male and female, are guided by their natural spirit. An apparent reciprocal relationship exists between God and mankind. The Bible says that women will be preserved, saved, kept (depending on translation) through or in childbearing (1 Tim. 2:15). This statement reinforces that the potential to birth children is the one distinction between males and females. This difference makes her uniquely female and is an honorable distinction. Still, she must "continue *to live* in faith, love and sanctity with self-restraint" (I Tim. 2:15). In the Garden of Eden, the woman was beguiled into deciding in accordance with her natural inclinations instead of keeping the commands of God. Under the new covenant, once transformed by the Holy Spirit the restored nature directs choice and she will choose *in faith, love and sanctity with self-restraint.* Indeed the order of creation is significant. Woman came from man at creation and through childbearing man comes from a woman. Since *God does not show favoritism*, every person being equal can stand before the Almighty God (Rom. 2:11). Both male and female are directly accountable to the Creator. No spiritual class system or hierarchies exist therefore; neither of them can claim lordship over the other in any form. From the beginning relationship with God was to be acknowledged by the keeping of His commands. Unfortunately, Adam and Eve being the first humans in God's creation decided the pattern of relationship between God and men. In the garden, the serpent presented a paradigm that opposed the command of God. He offered appeals to their sensual nature, which was new to them, and to be as God persuaded their ego. How could they go against The Creator and accept the promptings of one of His creatures? Did God really say that they would die if they were disobedient? Did death mean the end? Perhaps they did not understand the truth. Opposition to the Word of God is the same as choosing a lie. Their spiritual development was affected at the pinnacle of decision. Adam and Eve had been given many gifts; the gift of life, to rule over all creation, the gift of choice and direct communication with God. Instead, for the two of them, having their own perceived power with minimal reliance on God was the ultimate gift, so they believed a lie and surrendered their distinctive identity. The lies that we believe impact our spiritual development.

Mankind was created with a free will as evidenced by the fall. According to Scripture, Adam was resolutely disobedient and Eve was independently deceived. Adam, who was given the responsibility to manage, was held accountable because of his decision to disobey God. Eve, as Adam's assistant, was held accountable because she was beguiled and therefore made the wrong choice. Although not appearing to be a thoughtful act of disobedience on the part of either individual, deliberation with the devil happened and from biblical accounts, consenting to Satan's falsehoods was the downfall of the deceived female. This does not mean that women are more inclined to deception. Since both the male and female are distinguishable components of each other it portrays the double-mindedness of humanity and God's inclusive punishment emphasizes His value of unity. Both were transgressors and both caused separation from God. For both the male and the female, God's Spirit was displaced by a nature-directed spirit. It is at the heart of the Christian that the attack is directed. In this instance the heart consists of the beliefs, the passion and the very character of the Believer. Mankind's view of its own humanness is where the assault from the world and Satan is directed. Each person has the capacity for choice and is bombarded with propaganda, philosophical, cultural and political agendas. Our society is filled with much rhetoric regarding human rights. People take a stand for human rights oftentimes to the detriment of justice, ethical and moral values. Although free will cannot be forced, it can be negotiated, coerced and manipulated. God looks down from heaven upon the children of men, to see if there are *any* who understand, any who seek God. The wicked in his proud countenance does not seek *God. God is* in none of his thoughts (Ps. 10: 4; 53:2). Whether our choices are weighed by our knowledge of God or not, standing atop the mountain and gazing over the edge searching for answers, safety and guidance our spiritual growth is influenced.

The king stood by the pillar and before God solemnly committed them all to the covenant: to follow God believingly and obediently; to follow his instructions, heart and soul, on what to believe and do; to put into practice the entire covenant, all that was written in the book. The people stood in affirmation; their commitment was unanimous.

II Kings 23:3, Message

CHAPTER FIVE

A Call to Commitment

Children of God must resist the dangerously false notions of errant concepts. The Bible teaches that there is only one Lord and underscores that faith manifested through Him is concretely real and pragmatic. Commitment is remaining steadfast, as one endures the trials and afflictions which befall disciples of Christ. Christians are to be committed in their faith. As Paul wrote, "having been justified and introduced into God's grace by faith, we are to exult in hope and in our tribulations, knowing that tribulation *achieves* perseverance; and perseverance *accomplishes* proven character; and proven character *produces* hope, and hope does not disappoint" (Rom. 5:1-5; emphasis mine). The cliff hanger by its very nature stresses the significance of Jesus as sovereign Lord. Initiation of relationship with God, as revealed in Scripture, requires identification with Jesus Christ who is God's agent in creation and redemption (Col. 1: 3-23). Faith is the cord that confirms commitment to this relationship. In Christ is all knowledge and wisdom. For every Believer, the choice to follow Christ is the beginning; the primary of the many mountain top decisions. It is a promise, a pledge, a vow, an obligation, loyalty and dedication. It is a call to commitment because in spite of who we are and all of our efforts to separate ourselves from Him, God loves us. He loved us first (I John 4:19). He loved us when we did not know Him or care about Him. He loved and pursued us when we were unfamiliar, unconcerned and unappreciative of His plan for our lives. God demonstrates His commitment. From the beginning of mankind's creation He has never forsaken His children. One of the greatest ploys of Satan is to cause people to disbelieve or to cause Believers to waiver in their belief of God's commitment, leading to losing sight of our own commitment toward God. We are admonished by the Word of God to pursue God and His righteousness as He pursues us (Luke 12:31).

Our call to commitment is represented as our obedience. Spurgeon exhorts, "to believe Christ and to obey Christ is the same thing; so as we read the Scriptures the same word that might be read believe might also be read obey."[26] The Bible expresses that the demands of discipleship are so arduous and obligatory that obedience instigates conflict within families; even opposition from parents, though the commandment of God emphasizes loyalty toward parents. Expressly, the first of the Ten Commandments contends that devotion to God take precedence over all worldly obligations and affections. According to the Scriptures, commitment is demonstrated as disciples, of necessity, share in Jesus' suffering (Mat. 16:24-28). Relationship with Him exacts that disciples accept that they will also receive the persecution and stigma attached to Jesus and must "deny thyself" which means to accept the assignment of death to the natural life with its rationalizations and sought-after success (Matt. 10:32-39). It means that the ultimate goal is to declare like Paul: "I count all things to be loss in view of the surpassing value of knowing Christ Jesus my Lord . . . that I may know Him and the power of His resurrection and the fellowship of His sufferings" (Phil 3:8,10). Therefore, careful calculations must be made regarding the demands of the kingdom of God because acceptance of the inheritance as a child of God requires absolute commitment. "God is not mocked," which is an assurance that He gets the glory (Gal. 6:7). To attain the fullness of life, which is observed as spiritual maturity, each cliff experience offers opportunity for renewal, sustaining power and to be built up in love (Col. 2:2; 3: 14).

In the Book of Genesis, God promised Abram that the number of his descendants would be as great "as the dust of the earth" (Gen. 13:6). He was 75 years old. In Chapter 15, Abram (Abraham) demonstrates his unrest with having no children, particularly no male heir to inherit and advance his lineage. God made a covenant with Abraham. He is told by God that he would have a son, "one who shall come forth from your own body" will be the heir of his house and again, that the number of his offspring would be too many to number" (Gen. 15: 4-5). Abraham had always demonstrated unwavering faith and yet, as the years passed without Sarah becoming pregnant, the two found themselves at the metaphorical cliff's edge. Predicated upon their concept of the allotted time, the promises of God had not been fulfilled and the need for a child became more persistent, overriding patiently waiting on God. At the crest of the mountain a decision was made that has affected the lives of many. As Abraham considered what the Lord had promised, he pondered God's covenant, his understanding of what was said and the time which was critical. So, *after ten years* and still childless, he and Sarah took matters into their own hands. She devised a means to conceive a child by arranging the consummation through her maidservant Hagar, and Abraham conceded. Although her strategy enables Abraham to have a son whose name is Ishmael, the plan of God was to be revealed according to God's timing. Abraham was informed that he and Sarai (Sarah) would become parents. His wife, Sarah would bear a son and he shall be called Isaac, and God would establish an "everlasting covenant with Isaac for his descendants" (Gen. 17:19). The name Isaac means laughed or laughter in Hebrew, mirroring Sarah's reaction, an outward sign of glee or disbelief, to God's pronouncement that they would have a child when they were very old. Fourteen years following the birth of Ishmael, when Sarah was ninety years old and Abraham was one hundred years old, Sarah bore Isaac. Isaac was the designated heir regardless of his birth order as Abraham's second son. Unbelievably, Abraham wavered in commitment to God during this cliffhanger experience. The desires of the natural man to have a son outweighed his spiritual wisdom to wait on the provision of God. The demand was so overwhelming that he might have convinced himself that to manipulate circumstances by his own efforts was by God's design. Evidence that this experience impacted Abraham's spiritual growth can be seen during his assignment to sacrifice Isaac. Again, Abraham would be challenged at the edge of the cliff. His previous blunder to manipulate circumstances wrought an increase in his spiritual prowess producing an enlightened Abraham who expected God to fulfill his promise of innumerable descendants and he unquestionably proceeded to perform the required task. Each cliffhanger is a reminder that if we do as God commands the responsibility of the matter no longer rests with us. Realizing and accepting this is a sign of spiritual growth.

The Bible indicates that although awaiting the presentation of a Messiah, even in the original historical Jewish society as well as for those that accepted Jesus, following Jesus would not bring peace to a family, but, "split" it up, which is the precise function of His statement regarding a metaphorical sword (Mat.10:34; Luke 14:25-33;). The faith of Christians can sever ties to non-Christian relatives, friends and neighbors; and causes stress for Believers, as it is tested through suffering and trials inflicted by the evil one. Are Christ's disciples ready for that? This kind of spiritual sword invisibly and sometimes irreparably strips a man from his father, and daughter from her mother, and so on (Micah 7:6). Given Jesus' own family's resistance at the onset of His earthly ministry, it is understandable that He would say, regardless what the cost, a disciple must follow Him to the end, even if it means giving up loved ones (Luke 14:26-29). But this division applies only toward the family that rejects the Believer, not those who accept the Christian's faith; those who are brothers or sisters in Christ with them. Christians must be mindful not to reject new converts, because the purpose of Jesus' advent is gaining people who will follow His example and become heirs of God's kingdom. Outlined in the Scriptures are key functions of church representative leadership: pastor, teacher, prophet, evangelist and apostles. Each has the assigned responsibility as leaders to equip the saints for the work of God (Eph. 4:12). Disciple-making is the primary goal of Christ even if it divides the world and according to Matthew 28:19, it should be the primary goal of the committed Christian; the body of Christ. "Awake you who sleep, arise from the dead, and Christ will give you light" (Eph. 5:14, NKJV). The call to commitment always takes you further than you think you want to go and teaches you more than you already know.

Leadership

Be on guard for yourselves and for all the flock, among which the Holy Spirit has made you overseers, to shepherd the church of God which He purchased with His own blood.

Acts 20:28

Every mountain top adventure includes the experience of peering over the edge recognizing that you must come down. At the edge of the cliff there is no turning around. It is here that you are stripped of ego and the concerns of this world. You are simply faced with the current condition you are in and stimulated to make the best judgment. There is a certain amount of exposure to risk that all mountain climbers face. The weather conditions are significant as they are unpredictable and can be frigid and wet, placing strain physically, emotionally and mentally. Most of all for leaders, the time of decision means awakening to the importance of living according to the will of God. After all, a leader must experience what it is like to follow and to be a good follower. Leadership makes decisions for themselves and others. Christian leaders: mothers, fathers, elders, pastors, teachers, prophets, evangelists and apostles may be responsible for a specific demographic or institutions established without boundaries. They have the duty of disciple making, training and empowering. The uncertainty on the mountain cliff and the unpredictability of the weather conditions are often apparent as leadership attempts to implement directives in the wake of opposition to personal perspectives, ideologies and traditions. The duty of leadership in every Christian assembly is to guide by biblical principles and its intention rather than emotion. Christian leaders are to be the example which requires commitment to the Word of God, discipline to manage oneself above reproach and effort to attain the desired result of developing disciples for kingdom building. Christian leaders are to be the ideal stewards in God's design. According to the deeds of Paul, leaders are to:

> Speak as those approved by God to be entrusted with the gospel; not trying to please people but God, who tests *the* heart. They are *required by Him* never to use flattery, nor put on a mask to cover up greed, or look for praise from people. Like Paul, Christian leaders are to be apostles of Christ, having authority but instead, behaving like young children, caring for God's children just as a nursing mother cares for her children; and because of love, delight to share not only the gospel of God but *their* lives as well. I Thess. 2:4-8

The requisite of one in authority is to feed God's flock like a shepherd and gently lead the nursing ewes (Is. 40:11). Those in authority must function as a counselor and director; as one who has received knowledge, wisdom and is just. Proprietorship should not be an aspect of their behavior, for "what *does anyone* have that *we* have not received?" (I Cor.4:7). The practice of parenthood is an analogy which reveals that once children arrive at maturation or adulthood, the parent's authority is not diminished. The parent still holds entitlement to the position and it is conceivable to receive acknowledgement, honor, respect and love. However, the role and status are changed which means that the parent no longer has power, dominion or responsibility for the child. This transition, which is often gradual, evolves into one that is more supportive and restrained to allow the child to grow and to become established as a leader in one's own right. Mentorship is another analogy for the expectant roles and responsibility of leadership. A mentor is the leader in a relationship of trust whereby the mentee is under authority to be guided, nurtured and equipped for a time specified often by development and maturity. At which time the mentee is liberated from the mentor's jurisdiction. The foundational message of the Bible regarding stewardship is that individuals are granted permission and given restricted authority to instruct, supervise and manage the things that belong to God. God owns everything. Everything and everyone belongs to Him. All of humanity are children of God and are to be servants of the Most High. Christian leaders have been given the assigned responsibility to evaluate themselves and their constituents within the body of Christ according to the biblical perspective of stewardship, along with accountability, when deciding how to utilize God's resources for the purposes of God. Every leader must be contained by God's will to avoid the elusiveness of the cliff and in order to realize their task as enabling the spiritual growth of another which is necessary for a leader's maturation.

After Jesus' ascension, in Acts 10:1-11:18, Peter, an apostle and a leader in the Christian assembly, was requested to meet with a prominent member of the Gentile community. Prior to this summoning, he had a vision where he was instructed to *kill and eat* animals, reptiles and birds, which was unlawful by Jewish principles. He was directed by God to accompany Roman visitors *without misgivings.* Awaking from the vision and perplexed, Peter pondered its meaning. He was faced with pending uncertainties. The vision presented an ultimatum "do not call unclean what God says is clean," and now Peter was required to blindly participate on an unknown excursion, *without misgivings.* What was he being prepared to encounter? Without misgivings meant, no apprehension, no second guessing, no fear; just faith. His own perceptions had been challenged and as the Christian leader, his will had to be guided by God's will; *what God says.* As he strove to the door he had come face to face with his cliff experience. He knew that God had given him an assignment that he must follow. Ready to comply with the Lord's command, Peter opened the door and invited the Roman strangers in. Through this lesson of obedience and self-sacrifice, Peter affirms "that God does not show favoritism but accepts from every nation the one who fears him and does what is right" (Acts 10:34-35). Did Peter maintain the respect of his colleagues by pursuing what was considered in his Christian circle as adverse to God? He did not receive popularity in their sight but Peter knew that his reputation was far less important than the mandate of God. At the cliff's edge he knew, that despite tradition, ethnicity, culture and doctrinal distinction, which were all wrought with dissension, leadership requires removing the intrigue so that God's grace shall prevail.

The most likely to succeed is the caption under your picture in the high school yearbook. You graduated from college with honors, married a fine woman and became the father of two children. You are proud of your accomplishments. Everything you have is because of your good decisions and hard work. Nobody has ever given you anything. People recognize and admire you. Your achievement has always been your number one priority. The executive job, with its high salary and the brand new house with every imaginable amenity is because of you and you alone. With your words you testify that God has blessed you but in your heart and when aroused you state emphatically that success came by the works of your hands, your astuteness and your ability to plan. Despite the often unstable marketplace and anxiety-fused people that surround you, you find solace by taking inventory of your possessions. You have even decided to catalog items for insurance purposes, although it is just another way to bask in the fruit of your accomplishments. Then the unexpected happens. There is a threat to every material thing you have. A health catastrophe or job loss could cause an extreme shift of fortune. A good reputation which has been tarnished or destroyed by the media; or a brush with the law can shift your lifestyle. Whatever the situation, your primary concern is to hold on to everything you have earned because nothing is more important than fame and fortune. While ascending the mountain, you never expected to have to choose between your prosperous life and the common existence that is now looming before you. Infidelity has caused a tidal wave in your life. Being the leader and having authority is not all-inclusive. It does not mean lording over another or, using an old adage, "do as I say and not as I do." It does not include disrespect or subordination. Christian leadership is to be sustained by the Holy Spirit and therefore epitomized by "love, joy, peace, forgiveness, kindness, faithfulness, self-control, long-suffering, and goodness" (Gal.5:22). The road you have been traveling has abruptly come to an end. What went wrong? The inevitable outcome is that you will lose income, resources, house and all your fanciful things. Your way of living will drastically change. You have always, with all arrogance, been the captain of your ship and now you are the crewman. The life story of kings Nebuchadnezzar, Herod and David represents different views regarding pride and arrogance; and the message of the cliff as an illustration of impending consequence from God. When Nebuchadnezzar reflected upon his accomplishments, he reveled in his "greatness" concluding: "I have built Babylon as a royal residence by the might of my power and for the glory of my majesty?" (Dan. 4:30). As he spoke these words aloud, the Lord declared to Nebuchadnezzar that there would be consequences for his choices and therefore, "Immediately the word concerning Nebuchadnezzar was fulfilled; he was driven away from mankind, began eating grass like cattle, and his hair grew like eagles' feathers and his nails like birds' claws" (Dan. 4:30-33). After a time his "eyes were raised toward heaven; reason returned, so he blessed the Most High, praising, exalting and honoring the King of heaven, for His works are true, His ways just, and He is able to humble those who walk in pride." The proud and arrogant King Herod, donned in royal apparel and seated "on his throne delivered a public address to the people who shouted, *This is the voice of a god;* immediately, because Herod did not give praise to God, he was struck down, eaten by worms and died" (Acts 12:21-23). Alternatively, King David believed, trusted and loved God, and being humbled by His greatness gave homage to Him and declared that "both riches and honor come from you and you reign over all; for all things come from You, and from Your hand we have given You as sojourners before You, and tenants" (I Chr. 29:11-15). In spite of popular opinion, there is no honor in arrogance. You are reminded of this as you survey the darkness beneath the cliff. "Pride goes before destruction and a haughty spirit before a fall" (Prov. 16:18, NKJV). It is here that you stand face to face with your insignificance. At the cliff, another decision is required of you. Your cliff experience is to bring you to the realization of your minuscule part in the grand scheme of your life. You have no control but, inevitably you must choose understanding, acceptance, forbearance and repentance. Understanding means knowledge, familiarity or a state of cooperation with a particular thing or relation between people. Acceptance is the favorable receipt of something offered; the act of assenting or believing. Repentance is demonstrated as deep sorrow for wrong which causes a complete reversal of perspective, attitude and behavior. Forbearance is defined as restraint, conduct of patient endurance or tolerance. Neither of these will return your material possessions or idealized reputation, but may offer spiritual regeneration and a renewed mind for transformation.

The First Book of Samuel emphasizes that the success of leadership is determined by devotion to God and His appointment, not on personal giftedness, religious fervor or position. For example, Saul was the first appointed king of Israel. He had the respect of the people and the jurisdiction to maintain the laws of God. His hapless concern for the intimate relationship that God requires, blinded him to his stark disobedience to the commandments of the Lord. His moment on the cliff and time of decision came when he and his soldiers sequestered the king of the Amalekites and the spoils of their defeat. Saul had been directed by God, through the prophet Samuel, to war with the Amalekites. He was instructed to destroy them all, along with their possessions. Instead he spared the king of Amalek and kept what was considered valuable in men's eyes. Confronted with the facts, Saul sought remedy by craftily explaining to Samuel that the decision was made by the army to honor the Lord with the choice spoils (I Sam. 15:20-21). Saul appears ignorant of his own contrariness and the omniscience of God. In any organized effort, accountability of the assignment rests with leadership and in the kingdom of God commitment to God's Word is the ultimate obligation. Placing anything above God and His commandments, statutes and precepts is idolatry. "Had the Lord as much delight in religious traditions as obeying the voice of the Lord? (I Sam. 15:22). According to Scripture, Saul's aggression and pride exacerbated his "rebellion" which is compared to the pagan practice of "divination," and his "insubordination" a presumptuous sin akin to" idolatry" (I Sam. 15:23). Sacrifice is never superior to obedience and authority does not overrule principle; nor does *might make right*. Although Saul gives the appearance of religious enthusiasm and spiritual aptitude, the Lord challenges his results as iniquity and evil practices. Much like every leader, Saul had multiple options to choose from, though only one was right. At the time of decision on the mountain peak he redefined God's plan, did what was the desire of his own heart and ruled by self-righteousness rather than the righteousness of God. His cliff hanger experience altered the future he imagined for himself and signaled his eventual demise.

The charge of leadership is to empower constituency (Eph. 4:11-13). Christian leadership has the unassuming duty to assist in the journey of the saint. Accountable to God, leadership must be accommodating to reassure the saints of individual calling, often presenting varied opportunities to express and develop gifting. When leaders do not stay on task and perform the duties assigned by God, it is disobedience. In the Book of Luke chapter 12 verses 42 to 43 Jesus asks the question: "Who then is the faithful and wise manager whom his master will set over his household, to give them their portion of food at the proper time? Blessed is this servant whom his master will find so doing when he comes." Accordingly in Luke 12:41-53, leadership's main responsibility concerns people; having a genuine interest in their spiritual welfare. Jesus warned against self-absorption and losing sight of the Master's business. He implies that loss of focus produces misuse of power and negligent conduct. A wise leader is diligent and vigilant in the performance of duty; avoiding temptation. Individuals who ascertain the will of God and have been assigned leadership positions are responsible to obey His rules of engagement. Jesus recognized that controversies and arguments would occur and foretold that individuals attempting to usurp the authority of God would bring division, as all Believers are servants and as such must work for the Kingdom. According to Scriptures, both intentional disobedience and ignorance will be allocated the punishment arranged for an unbeliever as both instances are attributable to a disingenuous relationship with God (Luke 12:46-48). As it is written, "there should be unity in the body of Christ where there is only one Lord of all and one Spirit in all working through every Believer" (Eph. 4:4-6). The heart of humanity was exposed at the cross. Still today the heart continues to prefer division, strife, persecution and bloodshed. Christian leadership is tested throughout their time on the mountain. The assuring guidance by the Holy Spirit to direct fellow laborers of the Lord and to direct decisions according to the will of God, as expressed by the Word of God, are expected as the only way to seek definitive answers to the tough questions at the cliff's edge. For the Christian, an exercise in discernment, acquiring truth through prayer and searching Scriptures during the cliff hanger moment will affect the spiritual maturation of every saint including leadership, for good.

Apostleship

> *Therefore they said to Him, "What shall we do, so that we may work the works of God?" Jesus answered and said to them, "This is the work of God that you believe in Him whom He has sent."*
>
> John 6:28-29

According to text, the word apostle literally means "one, who is sent." It conjures one who is sent forth as a messenger and should not be confused with the meaning of a disciple who is a follower or learner. While all Believers are disciples, all are not apostles (I Cor. 12:27-31). Examples given for an apostle today are church planters and missionaries. The term, apostle, is usually associated with Jesus' twelve disciples, all of whom (except Judas, "the son of perdition," who was sent on a different assignment) went out to spread the Good News about Jesus after the Pentecost (John 17:12). Apostleship was entrusted to the first twelve disciples by Jesus. "Jesus called his twelve apostles to him and gave them authority to drive out impure spirits and to heal every disease and sickness; these twelve Jesus sent out as sheep in the midst of wolves" for the good of the body of Christ and to advance interest among men of His Kingdom (Mat.10:1, 16). They were the initial representatives, but Scripture does not indicate that apostleship was restricted to the original twelve disciples. Paul, Barnabas and others were included as apostles (Acts 14:4, 14; Rom. 16:7; I Cor. 9:1; II Cor. 8:23; Phil. 2:25; I Thess. 2:6). When the time came to replace the fallen disciple Judas, the entire body of Believers was consulted and invited to choose appointments (Acts 1:15-26). "The company of persons consulted was about 120 and they chose someone to join who were in their group during the whole time that the Lord Jesus traveled about with them, beginning from the time John preached his message of baptism until the day Jesus was taken up to heaven" (Acts 1:15; 2:21-22, NLT). The apostles could have identified and suggested additional members but a certain two were selected and the whole congregation, by the Holy Spirit, "cast lots" to vote them into the office (Acts 1:21-26). Scripture asserts that those who were chosen by the Lord to be with Him as apostles were "to be witnesses of His resurrection" (Acts 1:22). For some this statement directly limits apostleship to the days of Jesus as witness means to observe. However, witness also connotes informing, affirming and decreeing indicating that these apostles were to continue proclaiming the message about Jesus for the expansion of His Kingdom (Mark 3:14; Acts 1:21-22). The Bible states that although Believers since Jesus' ascension have not directly seen Him, because we believe the account of His eyewitnesses, we are witnesses (I Pet. 1:8). Therefore, indirectly all who believe are witnesses and therefore enabled to receive apostleship. Apostleship is often challenged and misunderstood. The assignment of the apostle is acknowledged in the Bible as pertaining to Christian leadership called to service in Christ's church (Eph. 4:11). Much like the original apostles of Christ, an apostle is given responsibility to lay the foundation of the body of Christ, to relay God's Word and to display confirmation of the Word of God through exhibited signs, miracles and wonders from Him who has sent them (Acts 11: 28; 21:10-11; II Col. 12:12; Eph. 2:20; 3:5; Heb. 2:3-4). The Bible states that all who believe "are no longer strangers and aliens, but fellow citizens with the saints, and of the household of

God *who* are built upon the foundation of the apostles, and prophets, *with* Jesus Christ being the chief corner stone" (Eph. 2:19-20). In Scripture, the designation of Barnabas, Silas, Timothy and others, as apostles, provides evidence that the assignment was not abolished following Jesus' earthly sojourn (Acts 14:4; Rom. 16:7; Phil. 2:25; I Thess. 2:6). Even now, "Christ Jesus is the corner stone in Whom the whole body of Believers, being fitted together, is growing into a holy temple in the Lord" (Eph. 2:20-22). God's capacities are limitless. By God's Spirit, adoption as children of God is a binding, sectarian relationship validated by His confirmation of spiritual gifts, the fruit He produces in and through us and the power He extends for spiritual service (Gal. 5:22-23; Acts 1:8).

Finding oneself in uncomfortable territory due to circumstances which have, for all practical purposes, been outside of your control incites internal conflict. However, despite this situation, you have decided to sacrifice personal comfort in favor of maintaining your relationship with God. God's call for the life of an individual in the spirit realm will always manifest in the natural realm. The Bible affirms: "The Holy Spirit testifies with our spirit that we are children of God and you shall know them by their fruits" (Rom. 8:16; Mat.7:15-17). As Jesus was sent on assignments by God, similarly Christian leaders, fellow heirs in Christ, have been sent and "indeed suffer with Christ," whether from mockery, persecution or ridicule and these "sufferings are not worthy to be compared with the glory that is to be revealed" (Rom. 8: 17-18). An apostle's experience on the cliff incites the use of discernment, prayer and searching of Scriptures to identify the call of God, to ascertain the course of action and to develop faithful perseverance to sustain through persecution, dishonor, and disdain. Whether an apostle, pastor, teacher, prophet or evangelist, a Christian leader has the authority of God and decision at the cliff's edge must promote the advancement of the intentions of the Divine.

Scripture urges us to "Be strong in the Lord and the power of His might; *and* take up the whole armor of God that you may be able to withstand in the evil day" (Eph.6:10, 13). We are provided with a political and military analogy in which to view our struggles and cliff events. In the context of the political and military aspects of leadership there is turmoil, perhaps far removed from individual spirituality in both perception and seemingly importance, informing that an impending transformation is underway. For thousands of years a power struggle has been taking place among various constituencies. These constituents are families, congregations, communities and administrations. As with all hierarchical arrangements, the outspoken group has maintained control regarding important issues, over territory, finances and governance. When several group members joined to oppose the most prominent decision making group, the group that had been in charge gathered allies for a vindictive attack. There are those who seek to remain an objective observer. The fallout between the two factions will be immeasurable, leaving you defeated with the others who have remained objective. You realize that all of you may become identified as hostages because of close proximity and any participatory communication without choosing sides. You believe that responding to both sides is necessary for a hopeful reconciliation. Living amongst those outside of the foundational group and trying to bring together divided perspectives has become more than you can bear. God has placed a great burden upon your heart for His people. Your efforts to establish a process that engages, supports, encourages and edifies each group reveal widespread antagonism. You and several others recognize that internal dissonance will only beget corrosion of the core and ultimately, the cohesiveness needed to maintain relationship will be abated. Surely, the capability to continue distinctly separated is a fundamental alternative, but this will eventually lead to total destruction identified as loss of respect, values, familiarity and closeness. Feeling that the journey has led you to the pinnacle of a cliff where decisions must be made whether to get involved and how to address the sensibilities and sensitivities of both groups, you realize that you as the objective center are worse off than the two dissonant factions on either side of you. Unlike many people, you find it difficult to accept the status quo, you are compelled, so you act. The decision to avert trouble indicates commitment to that which you are called despite obstacles, anxiety, maltreatment or the unknown. Forging ahead with the commitment of Esther, "if I perish, I perish," you know that the assurance of a positive outcome rests with God (Est. 4:16). You have grown to trust Him more each time. After the many obstacles, adversities and trials that He has helped you navigate on the mountains your commitment is strengthened.

Christianity is a commission to carry the gospel of the Word of God. The Bible also provides that Paul, the most recognized missionary in the early church, was called an apostle of Jesus Christ although he was not one of Jesus' apostles who had the distinction of receiving His teachings and witnessing His resurrection. In his writing to Timothy, there is reference to Timothy being an apostle to define his role in relation to Christ and being sent by Paul to the church at Ephesus (I Thess. 2:6; I Tim. 1:1-3). Paul's conversion and preparation for apostleship was ordained by God. Paul was to be supported and guided by one of Jesus' disciples, Ananias. This disciple was an adamant follower, whose faith and obedience was tested on his mountain peak. Paul, then Saul, met Jesus on the road to Damascus, after which he lost his sight. He was assisted on to Damascus. There he remained praying and received a vision from the Lord. Ananias was imparted aspects of the same vision from the Lord. He was instructed to go to Saul (Paul) and "lay hands on him so that he might regain his sight" (Acts 9:12). Ananias had to confront his own anger and fear concerning Saul. He had "heard terrible things this Saul had done to Believers" (Acts 9:33). How could he trust him? Is he going into an ambush? Is Saul really a Believer of the way or is it all a hoax? Ananias had to choose between his own apprehension, which he believed was rational, or faith and obedience that God would grant victory. He was being sent to fulfill the purposes of God, but would he regret it? Ananias was standing at his cliff's edge, responsible for leading another yet, caught in tradition, the natural inclinations of man and his own religious experience. While, seeking the Lord for an answer he heard the Lord say "go, for he is a chosen instrument to carry my name before the Gentiles, kings and the children of Israel" (Acts 9:15). So Ananias went and performed the duty the Lord required of him. His time on the crest of the mountain proved to expand his faith, and his choice was to follow Christ.

The apostolic office exists to make fully known the Word of God (Col.1:25). Following Christ's ascension, the apostleship involved evangelism, church establishment, training and administration. Through Christ every religious and social barrier dividing mankind has been broken to be replaced by unwavering devotion to Him (Col. 1:21-22; 2:7). When lives have been transformed by the creative, redemptive and restorative purpose of God, every political, social, cultural, racial and religious distinction is meaningless (Col. 3:11). Every Believer is a disciple of Christ who are called and sent according to the purposes of God. The one indisputable aim is to please God. While the Believer walks by faith, this life of faith is analogized in Scripture as a struggle akin to a battle or a competitive race (Eph. 6:12; I Cor. 9:24; II Cor. 10:3-4; Heb. 12:2). Apostleship is the acknowledgement of God as Lord expressed in a specified act of service subsequent to the call of God on one's life. Are you called? Acknowledging God as Lord means knowing and understanding that His purpose has become your aspiration. "Hear O Israel: the Lord, our God, the Lord is one!" (Deut. 6:4) The call to commitment requires that God commissions, directs, and provides the message that the Believer accepts unwaveringly and unconditionally. Tradition, theological assumptions and humanistic perspectives all are an affront to apostleship. These place additional weight on the capacity of the Believer to assume the responsibilities of apostleship which leads to the cliffhanger and is identified as constraint. For the Believer called to task in nontraditional environments there is tension to address the demands of the commission. The only clear path to spiritual maturation is to seek God and relationship with Him irrespective of earthly circumstances.

Christian Love (AGAPE)

Tend my sheep. John 21:15-17

Jesus told Peter, if he loved Him to take care of His disciples. The Apostle Peter is described in literature as an uneducated fisherman (Acts 4:13). Theologians, scholars and Bible teachers attribute the characteristics of being impulsive, inquisitive and impetuous to him. Peter as the rock of the church was assigned pastoral ministry of Christians. His assignment was to care for the Believer's spiritual, emotional and mental health, outline proper conduct, and establish the necessary resources to construct and maintain relationship with God and each other. Peter was the disciple given understanding, by the Spirit of God, concerning the foundation of the Church which is "Christ, the Son of the Living God" (Mat. 16:16). The Word of

God provides narrative of Jesus' assignment for Peter. During a discussion Peter promises to always stand with Jesus yet; Jesus tells Peter that when the time of testing comes, He will act contrary to this commitment. Jesus knowing the heart of Peter and seeing God's Spirit at work in him, maintained high expectations regarding him and interceded on his behalf. Jesus gave Peter the obligation to strengthen his fellow Believers following his cliffhanger experience (Luke 22:31-34; 54-62). When the occasion on the cliff arrived, Peter denied the Christ three times which was unimaginable to him when Jesus foretold the incident. What made Peter deny Jesus? What was he thinking? Was it fear for his life, Christ's life or both? Was it concern for his reputation? Was he preoccupied with the things of this world? Peter wept, realizing that despite his complete denial of the Lord, he was forgiven and assigned the responsibility of leadership. Because he was shown grace, Peter encouraged eternal security in the life of the Believer, exhorting that past sins are forgiven, the present is protected and the future is assured (I Pet. 1:4-7). After his time on the cliff, Peter resolved to express his love for God and relationship with Him in practical terms. The culmination of his time on the cliff presents this disciple of Jesus Christ equipped to live in the natural world where faith is tested and tried, committed by having the spiritual world in view by maintaining a heart on fire with love for the Master (John 21:1, 15-19; I Pet. 1:8).

Peter was a leader, an apostle, a disciple of Christ, a man and a servant of the Most High God. Jesus gave him the command that if he loves Him then he must show love for the disciples of Christ. Leadership is not exempt from the imperative of I Corinthians 13. It states: love suffers long which means patient endurance especially under provocation. Love is kind. Kindness is demonstrated as goodness expressed in the interest of others. Love does not envy but is pleased with the accomplishments of others. Love does not parade itself, it is not puffed up. It is showing appreciation for others; even the consideration for the care received from others recognizing that all gifts are bestowed from God. Therefore, nothing exists in this life that should cause us to become haughty or proud. Love does not behave rudely but is courteous and considerate. Love is other-centered and not selfish, self-centered or self-seeking. It is not provoked, but willing to remain humble; existing for the Lord. Love does not *sweat the small stuff.* It does not assume the worst. It is sincere, honest and straightforward. It does not take pleasure in another's ill-fated circumstances or any unrighteous actions which benefit another. Love firmly gives godly discipline. It does not publicize faults. It attempts to guide in the direction of faith and fairness; and earnestly desires that things work out for the good of all. Love is forgiving and attempts to understand those it loves. Faith, hope and love are all virtues which should be sought after persistently and exercised purposefully by all disciples of Christ. Faith is commitment to the attributes of God and His all-sufficiency. Hope is the anticipation of an expected end of promises kept, "for the good of those that love the Lord" and respond to His summons, acting "according to His purpose" (Rom. 8:28). Love, godly benevolence, which is also translated as charity, is the "greatest of these" virtues (I Cor. 13:13). Love has the most value relative to a Believer's behavior towards others. By this love, Christian leaders are held responsible for the welfare of others, it binds the spirits of all redeemed, every Believer's will with God's will and unites each creature with The Creator. Paul reinforces that beneficence, being useful to others without recompense correlates to God's grace. Therefore, for the Believer, God's grace is a call to commitment through love.

Christ's presentation of Agape love to Peter is an instruction in the difference between enamored love for a lover or friend and the unhindered love that God requires amongst His family. The assertion is that it should be a willful choice with a conscious focus on personal spiritual growth and for the spiritual growth of others (*feed my sheep*). The Bible lists the characteristics of Agape love as patient, kind, accepting, limitless, trusting, enduring, hopeful, other-centered; it overlooks, bears and covers faults and mistakes, it is confidential, unselfish (*not seeking its own*) and benevolent. These attributes are often contrary to human nature and all require a conscious choice. The entire Bible expresses that mankind has freedom of choice. According to I Corinthians chapter 13, love has choice as its foundation. God in His infinite wisdom, mercy and grace exhorts every Believer to contend diligently for faith, maturity and unity of the Spirit that our Father's promise may be revealed (Eph. 4:1-16; Jude 1:3). Our heavenly Father shows us love exhibited as salvation through restoration. Our acceptance and ensuing compliance is voluntary. He does not force this love on us. We must choose this love; then we will receive the spiritual power needed to conquer failure, caused by our separation from this love, in our earthly lives (Luke 24:46-49; Acts 1:7-8). We must recognize this love as God's provision. The design for Agape love is further expressed in the narrative of the Good Samaritan (Luke 10:25-37). Jesus admonished those listening, to love their neighbor. When asked who was to be considered one's neighbor, He told the story of a traveler who had been beaten, robbed and in need of help along a well-travelled road. Many people passed by, specifically religious leaders, but only a Samaritan stopped. Noticeable in the narrative is that more than the immediate need was met; not only was the person assisted while out on the street, but the Samaritan assured his full recovery by making a commitment to the final outcome. All of us are simply mountain travelers and as such will find ourselves at the edge of a cliff. Remember those who were religious knew every letter of the law, even questioning Jesus about who to love asking, *who is my neighbor?* They were already aware the Scriptures admonish to love your neighbor as you love yourself (Leviticus 19:18). According to *The Five Love Languages*, when an act is not an instinctive response, it is a greater expression of love.[27] Love is something done for someone else even when it does not come naturally. With love, actions precede perspectives. Certain actions are chosen for the benefit of our loved ones. Remember that Jesus did it! "Thus it is written, it was necessary for Christ to suffer and to rise from the dead the third day" (Luke 24: 46). The divine power of love is often realized during the times of peering over the cliff of decision, garnering, as I Corinthians 13:8-11 suggests, a natural development toward spiritual development and maturity.

A Christian's first command is to love God, with all heart, mind and soul; and since this is how we love ourselves, it is to be demonstrated as the same love for the brethren (Mat. 22:37). The Word of God asks "how can you love God whom you have not seen and hate your brother whom you see? (I John 4:20). Paul asserts that the relationship to be exhibited amongst Believers is one of community. He emphasizes that diverse services are to be rendered by various people for the common good. Believers are urged to care for and share fully with each other. While he explains the graciousness of God to distribute gifts among the brethren, Paul espouses that the supreme gift, which is "the more excellent way," heralded from thc Spirit is love (I Cor. 12:31). This love should anchor each Believer to one another. This is demonstrably a call to commitment for every Believer as each is commanded to "pursue love, and desire earnestly spiritual gifts which are of no value without it (I Cor. 14:1). During times of testing their faith to believe God for His provision, Christians are often at the edge of the cliff. Do we always demonstrate the love that we read about in I Corinthians 13 toward Him and others, or is it only adopted when troubles arise and our expectations are turning to disappointment? The Word of God says "the testing of faith works patience" and "in due season we will reap if we faint not" (James 1:3; Gal. 6:9). The cliffhanger raises profound questions about our commitments and priorities. It is a lesson concerning how we participate in God's purposes and how faith is expressed through our life's events and relationships. During this spiritual experience of the cliff, one can anticipate the eternal benefits which result from faith or become bound by the expected weight of unspeakable labor and an unknown future expressed as burdensome trials and sacrifices. The cliffhanger tests our call to commitment of faith while constructing spiritual maturity through the revelation of Christ (I Pet. 1:7).

As the Book of Job illustrates the blessedness of the righteous, it also depicts the disconnect leading to destruction of the wicked. Readers are given a glimpse behind the veil into the spirit realm where the shroud of darkness surrounds every naturally sinful human. The question has been posed many times as to how a loving God could offer His most righteous Believer to Satan. Job 1:8 states: "and the Lord said to Satan, have you considered my servant Job?" The first instinct of natural man is to blame God. Scripture says Job was righteous, but so were Adam and Eve before their fall in the Garden of Eden. In the case of Adam and Eve, the blame is not directed at God because it is presented as a choice. However, let us be reminded that an all-knowing God foreknew the decisions of each of them even before the offer was made to choose between obedience to God and their own way. The Creator, God, and loving Father of mankind, had prepared a way even before creation of the garden for mankind's recovery, in Jesus. The Book of Job presents a foreshadowing of the salvation of God. Job's suffering, pain, and loss were a means of saving his wife, family, friends; and himself. Job was preoccupied with his prosperity and his restitution through sacrifice may have been the result of this preoccupation and the reason he was singled out (Job 1:3-5; 29:1-30:1). Recall the religious discourse of self-righteousness and pride; and the call to blaspheme from the well-meaning and in his wife's case, the loving. Job continued in his faith despite the enormous cost and like Jesus wanted this heavy burden removed, but only if it were the will of the Lord. The Bible addresses the turmoil that was going on in his mind. Am I to lose my happiness and prosperity which I have been fearful to lose? (Job 3:25). In my striving to walk upright, can a mortal be more righteous than God? (Job 4:17). Amidst this uncertainty, am I able to trust the wisdom, love and power of God? (Job 19:6) Job, though righteous in God's sight, was still a man. A sinner saved by God's holiness and sanctification. His cliffhanger was to stay attuned with God, to abide in Him amidst the arrogance, pride, strife and dissension, against torrid remarks and ideologies that tried to disengage him from the Truth. Similar to Jesus, Job was sacrificed for love. Job's call to commitment and ensuing response seems to be different from Adam. His does not appear as a fall but an offer. His plight is not fair by human standards, but look at it through the lens of a loving, merciful Father who wants all of His children to survive. Job attempted to please God by his righteousness through laws and traditions; and discovered that "he was righteous in his own eyes" (Job 32:1). However, when called upon he proved that without love for God, strivings about the law are unprofitable and vain; and "righteousness is as filthy rags" (Titus 3:9: Is. 64:4-6, KJV). Shall one who contends with the Almighty correct Him? (Job 40:2). Would you condemn God that you may be justified? (Job 40:8) Look at the response of Job. He states: "I have heard of You by the hearing of the ear; But now my eyes see You. Therefore, I abhor myself and repent" (Job 42:5-6). Even Job's encounter on the cliff wrought spiritual transformation. Job received this instruction in commitment from the Lord, "indeed the river may rage, yet he who is committed loves the Lord and is not disturbed. He is confident though the Jordan gushes into his mouth" (Job 40:23). Job was rewarded for his spiritual commitment and enlightenment. For the Christian the reward for commitment is belief, faith and safe return to the Father. This offers is for all who accept the Gospel. For it is written:

> For the Law, since it has *only* a shadow of the good things to come *and* not the very form of things, can never, by the same sacrifices which they offer continually year by year, make perfect those who draw near. Otherwise, would they not have ceased to be offered, because the worshipers, having once been cleansed, would no longer have had consciousness of sins? But in those *sacrifices* there is a reminder of sins year by year. For it is impossible for the blood of bulls and goats to take away sins. Therefore, when Jesus came into the world, He said,
>
> Sacrifice and offering you have not desired, but a body you have prepared for me; in whole burnt offerings and sacrifices. For sin you have taken no pleasure in them. Then I said, 'BEHOLD, I HAVE COME (IN THE SCROLL OF THE BOOK IT IS WRITTEN OF ME) TO DO YOUR WILL, O GOD.'
>
> He establishes that by His will we have been sanctified through the offering of the body of Jesus Christ once for all. Every priest stands daily ministering and offering time after time the same sacrifices, which can never take away sins; but He, having offered one sacrifice for sins for all time, SAT DOWN AT THE RIGHT HAND OF GOD, waiting from that time onward UNTIL HIS ENEMIES BE MADE A FOOTSTOOL FOR HIS FEET. For by one offering He has perfected for all time those who are sanctified. Hebrews 10:1-14

The message of Job is to bring encouragement. It is the rallying cry for numerous people who are at the edge of the cliff. Job's account expresses an undeniable truth, that when faced with much adversity the call is to commitment. A commitment is faith, hope and love; but the greatest of these is love (I Cor. 13:31). No longer was the God of the Universe placed in a box to provide according to religious traditions.

Job kept his commitment to God and received a revelation leading to spiritual growth in the process. His response was not only a commitment of faith; it was a commitment of love. God knowing Job's reaction from the beginning expected a favorable outcome and "the Lord restored the fortunes of Job increasing all that Job had twofold" (Job 42:10).

And do not be conformed to this world, but be transformed by the renewing of your mind, so that you may prove what the will of God is that which is good and acceptable and perfect.

Romans 12:12

Chapter Six

A Call to Change

The cliffhanger as a call to change may be the most difficult. It conveys a lifetime process of transformation. Each mountain journey is a time of discovery and each peak is a pivotal point for change. Sometimes change requires intervention, court-ordered treatment, financial ruin; and loss of employment, freedom, health and relationships. Many times we find ourselves reaching out to acquire social, medical and spiritual support to assist with the effects of change. Change brings us to the end of the self we think we know. There, at the end of ourselves, at the edge of the cliff, we often meet our spirituality. Spirituality offers a sense of life's purpose and its ultimate meaning; and a sense of connectedness with others. It is here that a deep concern for commitment to something greater than self is experienced. Here, there is an awareness, recognition and appreciation to search for wholeness in life. Spiritual beliefs, principles, ethics, values and fulfillment become most important. Interactions with others, characterized by personal relationship, compassion, trust, integrity, altruism, and service transcend normal observable physical reality. James 4:7 affirms that God wants humanity to submit to Him. Submission means to surrender or yield. At each juncture of the journey, at each cliff's edge, we discover that surrender is a way of life. Individuals are demanded by externalities to relinquish what is deemed personal control in the unanticipated circumstances of living. An externality is an external effect, often unforeseen or unintended, accompanying a process or activity. We are required to make choices which have negative and positive results. Wise choices can alter life for good, and foolish choices can be dreadful. We decide between hundreds of choices daily which seldom wrought lasting repercussions. Decisions generate change. Many times throughout our lives we become fragmented by the tyranny of our choices. Experiences in life call for good or bad decisions and challenge the status quo. Whether we are aware or not they help develop our spiritual being. Many often want to forget the bad choices that have been selected. Some cannot accept them, and unforgiveness is carried as a spiritual weight that places an insurmountable burden, spawning irrational thinking, resentment and all manner of untoward activities. The weight of unforgiveness prevents the process of spiritual growth which every cliffhanger brings. Still others try to change their experiences or pretend they did not happen at all, while harboring guilt, discontent and poor self-esteem. Each experience on the cliff is unique just as each individual is unique. We are who we are and we have survived our choices at the cliff, often in spite of ourselves. If we acknowledge the truth of our cliffhangers, we realize as humans we have a spirit that requires protection to be safe, guidance to be preserved from confusion and wisdom to be properly developed for good. If we would allow it, each moment at the cliff's edge will bring us closer to God. In some ways, the mountain peak is a moment of forced surrender and involuntary contrition. Even when the choice is to maintain the status quo; change happens. The cliffhanger is not an inconsequential event. Atop the mountain of decision spiritual development is confronted and *a call to change* is inevitable, but due to its complexity, spiritual development or growth is not always achieved.

Each cliffhanger is significant; never an inconsequential event. Placed in the care of a neighbor (maybe a foster home, childcare center, etc.), she was the youngest of several boys and girls who grew together, learned from one another other and demonstrated love, envy and apathy toward each other. One by one they all grew older. One boy was imprisoned for aggravated robbery, another became a singer-songwriter with opportunities to perform around the world. Two of the girls became mothers at an early age. One struggles to survive by any means, the other married; works, cares for her family and attempts to acquire a college degree. As they grew older, each of them had to make decisions from the choices they considered. She too, although the youngest, has been on the cliff many times. Grappling with religious teachings and unsettled sensual desires, she dabbles in various drugs and alcohol, has unprotected sex…frequently, clings to abusive relationships and becomes involved in many misguided alliances. Unable to keep a job, she exchanges sexual favors for money and makes many choices that are not so popular to the informed and judging. Somewhere in her life she decided that anything goes when it comes to living. Perhaps it is simply her own self-centeredness. She remarks to herself, *Thank God I have no children, I am not a drug addict and I'm still alive!* Having been spared, she has never considered the impact of her actions nor the possible and sometimes inevitable dangers. She is often alone, by herself to fend for herself, and makes choices based on her limited and narrowly conceived knowledge. She grew up expecting people to be honest and trustworthy but discovered they are deceitful and selfish. She has become bitter, despondent and despairing of her cyclical behaviors. How long can she live like this? She realizes that a change is necessary. Standing on the mountain peak, she ponders suicide. How did she get here? She was disillusioned by people. All people: mom, dad, brothers, sisters, pastors, teachers, friends, family, caregivers have been a disappointment. How can people be so cruel? There are difficult decisions to be made on the mountain peak. Some have to choose what to do with an unwanted pregnancy, unfaithfulness in marriage, desertion that leads to displacement, addictions or associations that lead to crimes. This wasn't the life that she envisioned. What was she searching for? Standing there at the crest of another mountain, she hears a voice say, "if you search for Me, you will find Me… learn of Me and you shall find rest for your soul. My yoke is easy…My burdens are light" (Jer. 29:13; Matt. 11:29-30). One day, she realizes that her life does not have to be over. It can be *just* beginning! She jumps off the cliff landing on the fluffy, soft wings of the ALMIGHTY. As she diligently, with her whole heart, and setting aside the previous life she knew, searches the Scriptures to find Him. She found herself.

According to the Word of God, every person is commanded to be confirmed, committed and changed; and to accept consequence and conflict. Each individual has a responsibility in the purposes of God and the whole body of Christ is expected to reinforce His nature by standing boldly in light of tradition, law, absurdity, pretense and vanity. Often the question of whether to follow God or tradition and culture is insoluble since most of our point of view resides there. Even in the worship of God, we categorically maintain that which we have always done. We can become stagnate, stubborn and self-absorbed. Despite circumstances that may necessitate change, the human need for an individually constituted reasonable amount of loyalty prevails. In effect, when loyalty and tradition supersedes the fact that there are Truths worth defending or ideas worthy of debate, then the very foundation of Christianity is at risk. Jesus queried many Jewish traditions and called for a reevaluation of loyalty. His contention was to render to the world what belongs to the world (Caesar) and to God what belongs to Him (Mat.22:21; Mark 12:17; Luke 20:25). The Word of God teaches that only one path leads to God which is considered by the majority of people in contemporary society to be a principle expression of personal preference. The call to change is fulfilled in the conduct of every person confronting the mountain peak. Scripture states that change involves a renewed mental process (Rom. 12:2). The Random House Dictionary states that change means to make the form, nature, content, or future course different from what it is currently; or would be if left alone.[28] In relationship with God and others we are transformed, the life of hysteria in which we live is quieted and the heart is renewed. The unbelieving, though not viewing the world so metaphysically, must align choices relative to the ability to ascertain the realities of life's situations, comprehend its precepts and distinguish future prospects. For the Believer, being a member of the universal body, the body of Christ, it becomes difficult to stand idly by and watch the spiritual defeat of God's people. While considerably challenged through conflict and consequence; and inhibited by tradition and loyalty, standing at the summit of decision it must become clear whether we are advancing the rule of Satan and contributing to the broken condition of the world or committed and confirmed to participate with God in transforming the world as His kingdom.

In the Book of First Samuel, God pronounces judgment on the entire house of Eli for his unwillingness to correct his sons for their transgressions. Eli was High Priest and judge of Israel at Shiloh, for forty years. His two sons were priests who were responsible to collect the sacrificial offerings according to custom. Eli learned that his sons were involved in treacherous practices. He rebuked his sons without consequence regarding their transgressions against God, so they continued with their evil behavior. Eli's sons, Hophni and Phineas robbed the offering by force, profaned the sacrifice to God and had intercourse with the women who volunteered service at the Tabernacle. Eli's failure to impede the improper conduct of his sons was irreparable in the eyes of the Lord. As the appointed leader, Eli was held accountable with his successors. God repeatedly declared this mockery to Eli and informed him of his personal responsibility regarding this matter. God presented many opportunities for restoration, enabling him to repent and do what was appropriate under the circumstances. Eli appeared unconcerned. The Lord said:

> I put your ancestral family in charge of all the sacrificial offerings of Israel. So why do you now treat as mere loot these very sacrificial offerings that I commanded for my worship? Why do you treat your sons better than me, turning them loose to get fat on these offerings, and ignoring me? (I Sam. 2:28-29)

Had Eli become complacent, thinking that God had appointed him and his family as priests without accountability or rival? How could God take the priesthood away from Eli which had been customarily given to his relatives since Aaron? As for his sons, the sacrificial meat is for their sustenance; could they help having such ravenous appetites? Did Eli fear his sons more than God? Would God really deny him after all of the time he has served Him? The dilemma left Eli perched at the edge of the cliff aware of the contemptible behavior of his sons whom he cared for deeply, knowing his responsibility as spiritual leader of the people and the example for his lineage to continue this assigned task; he wavered in his relationship with God. He was faced with a call to change. A change in behavior and a change in attitude would have an effect on his sons and future generations of his lineage. Eli's mettle was tested and he lost sight of the significance of adherence to the authority of God. The deplorable performance of his duty as the spiritual leader of God's people and as a parent, was the product of this discarded relationship with God which led to consequences. Although disappointments did not prevent God from making good use of Eli's life, and the same is true for each of us, oftentimes life does not turn out the way we would like yet, in the midst of our disappointments, God uses us and gives relevance to our lives that we do not expect. Eli's inaction to God's directive proved to be a decisive blow along his spiritual journey and resulted in his eventual physical demise (I Sam. 3:11-14; 4:14-18).

An Abiding Relationship with God

> *I am the vine; you are the branches. Whoever abides in me and I in him, he it is that bears much fruit, for apart from me you can do nothing.*
>
> John 15:5

The Bible is filled with examples of men and women the Lord used who faced the trials before them with initiative, boldness, and confidence. They stepped out in faith, relying on the provision of God and sensitive to the guiding hand of the Spirit. The human ability to trust God is based on previous instances in life but the Spirit of God within leads to an abiding relationship. In Strong's Concordance, the word translated abide is meno which means continuing in a permanent state and is attributed to words like: persevere, tarry, endure, remain, dwell and reside.[29] Jesus says, "Abide in me and I in you. As the branch cannot bear fruit except it abide in the vine; no more can you, except you abide in me" (John 15:4). Abiding is often expressed as the responsibility of the Believer to maintain coexistence with God. It is not determined by rules, religious activity or selfless dependence. However, considering the difficulty of mankind toward good, or the righteousness that God requires, Believers are tested to be continually operative in God through His divine influence. I John 4:13 states that we know that we abide in Him, and He in us, because He has given us His Spirit; and *the Spirit is given forever* (John 14:16). The Bible describes a permanent relationship with God in which we are to seek

His purposes for our life. The acknowledged permanency of this relationship involves a confident expectancy through circumstances based on experience, knowledge and trust. Every Believer, having received God's Spirit, learns to abide, depend on the Lord through our daily walk and trust in His providential care, especially during the pressures of life when the cliff's edge is encountered. The Holy Spirit gives us a *knowing* of the love of God and it produces confident anticipation which means *expecting* something special to take place. The relationship that has been developed over the testing of time, through knowledge and faith; and is based on past performance, endures and is faithful. We learn to count on God and in turn, by His Spirit, want Him to know that He can count on us. As we abide in our relationship with Him, we take captive every thought and strive with confidence, focused on God and what He is doing (II Cor. 10:5).

With each moment at the cliff, as a call to change, we are influenced to grow in wisdom. An abiding relationship with God discloses that life is lived as confidence in the wisdom of God rather than our own wisdom. Wisdom is personified or closely parallel with God himself as it speaks what is "true and just" (Prov. 8:6-7, NIV). God alone has knowledge and understanding of everything, therefore, gaining wisdom begins with a reverence for God. This is an abiding relationship with God; that the discerning accept all of His wisdom as "right and faultless" (Prov. 8:8-9, NIV). He desires to be heard by all, to impart His excellence and to make his intentions known publicly. Scripture states "wisdom cries out" (Prov.8:1). Wisdom cries out to everyone, bidding them to "live securely and at ease from the dread of evil" (Prov. 1:33). An abiding relationship connotes loyalty without compromise. It is characterized by humility (James 3:13-14). "Wisdom that comes from heaven is pure, peace-loving, considerate, submissive, merciful, gracious, impartial and sincere" (Prov. 8:17; NIV). Only God can give wisdom from heaven. Wisdom "is a spirit in man; and the breath of the Almighty gives them understanding" (Job 32:8). Wisdom from heaven is the applied knowledge of God as He is seen in the person of Jesus Christ. This godly wisdom is revealed through the Gospel and is fixed, by the Holy Spirit, in the Believer's heart. The result is assurance that reconciliation to God has occurred through faith in Jesus. Jesus portrayed that wisdom is more beneficial to others than the one who is wise. His wisdom was a blessing to all those around Him and remains so today. His death makes all Believers blameless. "How blessed are those, whose way is blameless, who walk in *godly wisdom* and seek Him with all their heart" (Ps.119:1-2; *emphasis mine*). The individual who diligently and prayerfully searches for Divine truth receives the capacity to discern events through the principles of godly wisdom which are "the fear and knowledge of God" (Prov.2: 5). As we seek wisdom, according to James 1:5-8, we must make our request with the self-assurance that God will grant what we require. The Word of God prepares us for trials, troubles and difficulties that bring us to the inevitable cliffs in this life. For example it says: "in the world you will have tribulation, but take courage; *My wisdom has* (I have) overcome the world;" *Lord,* "You, who have shown me many troubles and distresses will revive me again, and *your wisdom* will bring me up again from the depths of the earth" and lastly "consider it all joy, when you encounter trials, knowing that the testing of your faith produces endurance. And let endurance have its perfect result, so that you may be perfect and complete *in wisdom*, lacking in nothing" (John 16:33; Ps.71:20; James 1:2-4; *mine*). The implication is that God offers wisdom through the myriad of cliff experiences to develop the Believer's spirituality and elicit an abiding relationship with Him. When we are confronted by difficulties, we are experiencing the quintessence of the cliff, where engaging godly wisdom to determine our choices, instead of the normative use of worldly wisdom brings a call to change; and overcoming life's unrestrained atrocities builds character, strengthens resolve and promotes spiritual capacity and growth.

You have met the love of your life. Since your teen years, the two of you have been inseparable. You believe that God has designed you for each other and decide to marry after high school. Weathering the normalcy of maturity and married life; and navigating through the storms, you resolve to keep the covenantal promises the day you married in front of witnesses. Life has a way of challenging promises. There is an adage that says *that which does not kill you makes you stronger.* Circumstances of life can create a diverse perspective in the minds and hearts of a people bent on self-satisfaction, instant gratification and self-aggrandizement. Faith is often shattered when confronted by abuse in your relationship. Abuse can come in many forms and is recognized as your spouse has fallen prey to the desires of the flesh. This could be drugs (prescribed or not prescribed), illicit sex, exorbitant gambling or spending; and inattentiveness or whatever causes division within the household. In this case, to help the financial situation, the husband chose to sell illicit drugs. Eventually, the drugs were for personal use. Problems compounded, bills could not be paid, his choice of residence was always away from home and the truth left him. He became "desperately wicked" (Jer.17:9, KJV). Desperately, meaning in a manner of having lost all hope which is marked by, arising from, or showing despair; and wicked: having no evidence of the knowledge of God. After many years of tears, home in disrepair and attempting to maintain a semblance of respect. The wife and little children could no longer accept life as they knew it. Choosing to live apart from her covenant partner and trusting that God would take care of all things, did not separate her from the covenant that she had made all those years ago. Now, living on her own, was a young, attractive woman with several small children. She had the loving support of a praying mother and before long had employment to provide basic provisions for her family. Many tried to change her mind and heart so that her choice would be to turn away from the promise she had made at the altar and discard her abiding relationship with God. Yet, to the surprise of family and friends, whenever an opportunity arose, she would say: *God is going to save my husband and we will be together again.* When the children were in middle school and high school, the mom received a call. Dad wanted to come home to take his rightfully appointed position as head of the household. He had received help and believed the process of a relationship with God had begun because of the new steps he had taken. This was the answer to prayer and the confirmation the wife needed. The husband and wife had both reached a cleft of the mountain. As is the situation for everyone, each had to travel their road and come to this place individually accountable. Her husband considered his decision made and waited for the wife to choose. Although this day was expected by her spiritual being, her physical and rational being screamed against it. She found herself with so many questions relative to trust, fear, the children, the past and the future. She believed that the promise at God's altar was sealed by Him and "what God has brought together" no man, not even the actions of her husband could "separate" (Mat. 19: 6). Her decisions at the cliff's edge were based solely on her trust in God from the very beginning and the signs and wonders He showed her along the way. She jumped . . . . And even with the normal relationship issues; they remained contentedly in the covenant of marriage.

Quality relationships involve reciprocity. John 15:7 says "**If** you abide in me, and my words abide in you, ***then*** ask whatever you wish, and it will be done for you. Second Corinthians 9: 6 states **if** one "sows sparingly ***then*** *they* will also reap sparingly, ***if*** *one* sows bountifully ***then*** *they will* also reap bountifully. In Malachi 3: 10 God admonishes that **if** you "bring the whole tithe into the storehouse, ***then*** I will open for you the windows of heaven and pour out for you a blessing until it overflows." The Believer's abiding relationship with God is reciprocal demonstrated as trust, love, and acceptance of His timing; believing and acknowledging that God has proven to be most reliable. Although not contributing to our salvation, our reciprocity is also represented by our obedience, commitment to the Word of God, prayer and communion. When we encounter the many times of uncertainty and difficulty in this life, do we ask, how does the Lord want me to move ahead or do we bulldoze our way forward, expecting God to clean up our mess? Do we sit still and do nothing, waiting for the Lord to intervene? Or do we move out in faith, leaning not on our own resources but trusting upon the Lord and his provision each step of the way? A reflection on the beautiful Old Testament narrative of Ruth suggests that these are the same questions of which Naomi, Ruth, and Boaz must have contended. Naomi had to trust that God, upon their return to her homeland without male support, would ensure the future of her and Ruth. Ruth had to decide if she should go to an unfamiliar nation with different beliefs from her own or return to the comfort of her family and familiar gods. Boaz had to confirm that the relationship he sought with Ruth was appropriate in the sight of God. The aim of God is to bring His Kingdom to fruition; to create a spiritual revival in our lives. But restoration requires time and cooperation. Although life is filled with testing, trials and tribulations the cliffhanger event engages these moments of uncertainty which causes self-examination, evaluation of motives, attitudes, values, priorities and plans leading to lasting impressions on spirituality. The book of Ruth gives ample evidence that as the work of God advances, obstacles often emerge to interfere. This is true for our life as well. Often our trials are a result of forces beyond our control and sometimes they are of our own making. How we respond to these challenges reveals a lot about our faith and trust in the Lord. The story of Ruth is full of tradition, ritualism, culture, religiosity and laws. However, one significant aspect is that Ruth decidedly expressed her spirituality and desire for relationship with God, illustrating she had been given the faith which enabled her to set out on the path with Naomi in the first place. Her cliffhanger is evident and her spiritual growth is demonstrated in the follow-through.

During a time of famine, a man from Bethlehem, his wife Naomi, and their two sons left Israel and sought refuge in the neighboring pagan nation of Moab. While there, he died and his two sons married Moabite women, Orpah and Ruth. After about ten years, unexpectedly the two sons died, leaving all three women widows and without sons to care for them. The famine ended in Bethlehem and Naomi prepared to return there. The daughters-in-law had a decision to make. Orpah chose to stay with her Moabite family and gods, but Ruth demonstrated dependability and love for her mother-in-law by leaving with her and devoting herself to the *One True God* and the people of Israel. One day, while in Israel, Ruth ventured out to gather food. She happened upon the field of a righteous man named Boaz. Although a stranger, Ruth was welcomed by Boaz and invited to glean exclusively in his fields, thus providing for her and offering protection. Naomi had no male heir to maintain the family property or preserve the family name; and she and Ruth had no means to support themselves. Naomi sought security for Ruth and discovered that Boaz was a close relative of her family (Ruth 3:1). According to Israelite law and custom it was the responsibility of a near kinsman to care for or *redeem* female relatives. One way a kinsman-redeemer could help a childless widow in his family, was to enter into a levirate marriage (Deut. 25:5-6). Boaz was a kinsman of Naomi's dead husband, and so had a responsibility to assure that her condition was remedied. Naomi said to her daughter-in-law, "May he be blessed of the LORD who has not withdrawn his kindness to the living and to the dead. The man is our relative, he is one of our closest relatives" (Ruth 2:20). Naomi initiated a plan to persuade Boaz to act on their behalf. She was hopeful that Boaz would enter into a levirate marriage with Ruth to redeem them from both poverty and barrenness. He had already shown favor to Ruth, so Naomi seized upon what can be acknowledged as a God-ordained opportunity. She presented a detailed plan outlining how Ruth could influence Boaz into acting as their kinsman-redeemer. The boldness of Naomi's plan is considered shocking and immoral to many readers. After Boaz is filled with good food and drink, Ruth, adorned in nice clothes and perfumed, would lie down next to him at night. Naomi does not suggest anything immoral, but her plan gives the appearance of a choreographed effort to maximize Ruth's desirability and minimize Boaz's defenses. Naomi is expecting that fanning the flame of seclusion, opportunity and availability will ignite a fire that leads to marriage. Naomi was asking Ruth to take an initiative that is both daring and dangerous. A Moabite cannot be certain of the outcome of this venture or the moral acceptability in the community. How did she get in this predicament? Can Ruth remember why she came to this community of the people of God in the first place? Will Boaz act to save them from their desperate situation? What if Boaz rejects her or rebukes her for impropriety? What if he takes advantage of her sexually? What if nothing happens but people find out they spent the night together? After giving up all that she knew, including her own relatives and given such a risky plan, it would not be surprising at all if Ruth gave Naomi an outright refusal to participate in such a scheme. Ruth had promised that she would stay with Naomi and knew that this type of marriage was sanctioned by the Word of God so, Ruth did not refuse. At the cliff she says, "All that you say I will do" (Ruth 3:5). She was willing to put both her reputation and personal safety at risk to remain loyal to her original beliefs. Consequently, she entrusts herself to Naomi, to Boaz, and ultimately to their God who had become her God. And God rewarded her step of faith. She bore the child Obed and the stage was set for the future kings of the nation of Israel, and the coming of the Messiah, the King of kings; Jesus the Christ.

The Role of Hysteria

You will only look with your eyes and see the recompense of the wicked.

Psalm 91:8

Everything in our physical life opposes the transient existence and the eternal salvation of mankind. Although recognizing the reality of mortality, permanence is the pursuit and carnality is the obsession which provokes exaggerated behaviors and extreme quests. While seeking one's own desires of the flesh, separation from the Divine presence is realized. Many have heard of the seven deadly sins. The Seven Deadly Sins are: lust, greed, laziness, wrath, envy, pride and gluttony. The focus of the deadly sins is sensuality. Sensuality refers to feelings which have no foundation in reason or godly spirituality. It encompasses emotions, possessiveness, and covetousness. For many, since the majority of decisions are based upon the desires of the flesh, the varied choices in life can lead them into compromising positions. Everything that is done is based on an insistence on following one's own mind, making one's own decisions, doing what one feels like doing and what feels good to do. When the sensuality of man is allowed to dominate, people become "futile in their speculations, and their foolish hearts *are* darkened" (Rom. 1:18-23). The countless difficulties and disturbances in life can cause many to become bitter, self-centered and resistant, even toward people who are trying to help. When overcome by situations and perceiving them through a carnal lens, a change takes place that causes an unconscious proclamation of who we are at the very depth of the soul by the way we react to things that happen to us. The Word of God says, "Pursue peace with all *people,* and holiness, without which no one will see the Lord . . . looking carefully . . . lest any root of bitterness springing up cause trouble, and by this many become defiled" (Heb. 12:14-15, NKJV). The tendency of mankind is to rely on the desires of the flesh. When this occurs it suggests a wrong relationship with God. As previously noted, a wrong relationship with God causes disengagement of rational thinking because the individual has no connection with their source of existence. According to Oswald Chambers, the slothful indifference that gradually invades "an unhealthy soul, produces the physical madness of hysteria."[30] Hysteria is defined as excitement, agitation, delusion, foolishness, frenzy, insanity and panic. It is often represented by uncontrollable displays of emotion or expressions often characterized by irrationality. The disposition of hysteria is sensual stimulation allowing biological urges without limit and self-absorption. These give occasion to the devil and self-absorption leads to the influence of a strong personal desire, at the risk of losing efficacy in the purposes of God. Hysteria in our society is demonstrated as individuals push past necessity and practicality; and engage in the deception that there is a moral imperative to have what is desired. The state of mind is one of unmanageable excess, loss of self-control, lack of inhibitions, feelings of unreality and detachment. The need for healing and recovery becomes evident by the circular, repetitious lifestyle; the pendulum experiences demonstrated in the ecstasy and agony of life. The time at the pinnacle of decision presents opportunity for relief from an existence centered in hysteria. Individuals or cultures following the sensual nature instigate behaviors, and the observing group mimics them as demonstrated by the fallen nature of humanity. There is poorly functioning family, church and community structure, mass violence, sexual promiscuity and outbreak of disease. At the cliff's edge, this hysteria, which focuses on the sensual, is revealed to the child of God. Those who recover are bewildered that they acted so out of character. A relationship with God is indispensable. Without relationship with God, even the Believer makes personal use of God's grace and rationalizes events which are in opposition to the truths directed by the Holy Spirit (Heb. 10:29). Based on individual choice, the cliff hanger experience is significant to effect spiritual maturation for better or for worse.

How did you get here? You ask this question following the feeling of being awakened from dream-filled sleep. But you were not asleep. You were awake the entire time. It seems like it was all a dream because you could never imagine taking part in the things you have witnessed. How did you get here? Could you have said, "No?" Of course, you could have, but then you might not have received what you had considered to be *something good*. Something good like . . . a feeling, money, security; anything that satisfied your need of the present. You simply went along with the events as they progressed enjoying the time and basking in the adrenaline-produced moment with no thought of consequences. Even if you thought of repercussions, the thought did not take precedence over the here and now. *Let tomorrow take care of itself*, takes on new meaning when you are lavishing in transgressions. So what is it that has your mind entangled in darkness? Is it drugs, sex, violence, lust or scandal? Is it safety, security or the fear of loneliness? Whatever the particular self-absorbed behavior, it is evident that you are living recklessly. In fact, you are so reckless; you are not taking into account the affects you are having on others. When you really ponder your behaviors, would you want them mimicked by those you love; for instance your brothers and sisters, your sons and daughters? God has awakened you from that dream-filled sleep once again. How did you get here? You are standing on the tip of the cliff and observing nothing tangible. You cannot discern what is ahead by any of your senses. Yet, within the hysteria of your life, you are accosted for a decision. *Now,* the question is: How do I get away from here? The answer will promote your spiritual development. Remember, that you are created in the image of the Almighty God. There is power in your faith and you receive His power when you are in agreement with Him. Consider what God would say about your situation. "Walk by the Spirit, and you will not carry out the desire of the flesh. The flesh sets its desire against the Spirit and the Spirit against the flesh; so that you may not do the things that you please" (Gal. 5: 16-17). Think, according to God's Word, how He would want your life to be, and as you share the understanding that God gives to you with others, you begin to speak life to your broken dreams. Using the power of faith that God has given; keep an attitude of expectancy and as you do, God will take you places that you have never dreamed of. He "will give beauty for ashes, oil of joy for mourning, and a garment of praise for the spirit of heaviness; that you may be called trees of righteousness; the planting of the Lord that He may be glorified" (Is. 61:3). He will make something beautiful out of every broken place in your life; "for nothing will be impossible with God" (Luke 1:37). A call to change as a time of spiritual reformation and maturity is difficult because to choose a different road means stepping off the cliff of hysteria and becoming a spiritually "new creation" (II Cor. 5:17).

The role of hysteria may be observed during the life and times of King Solomon. He exhibited excessively intense interest and desire for grandeur. King Solomon was the third king, after David and Saul, and the last ruler of the twelve tribes of Israel. He was chosen by King David to be king, instead of an older son who, according to tradition, was expected to have been the successor. This caused considerable dissension before the *new king* was firmly established. Adonijah, David's oldest surviving son, proclaimed himself king with the support of various prominent individuals. The report of his rebellion reached an ailing and aging King David who ordered the immediate coronation of Solomon in response to Adonijah's imminent takeover (I Kings 1:5-40). Adonijah and his followers feared Solomon as king and were repentant. They were pardoned with concessions. Solomon later had Adonijah put to death for a plot to gain the throne (I Kings 2:25). On his deathbed, David gave parting instructions to Solomon, admonishing him to follow God's law; noting that on this command, God's promises to the house of David were dependent (1 Kings 2:1-9; 1 Chronicles 22:7-16). When Solomon began to reign as king, the kingdom "was firmly established (I Kings 2:12). Solomon ordered the building and dedication of Israel's first Temple of God in Jerusalem which remained their approximately four centuries. The Temple was to serve as a permanent place for the Levites to house the Ark of the Covenant that contained the Ten Commandments and to perform their other duties. After The Temple was completed, Solomon engaged in numerous other great projects throughout Jerusalem and Israel. Solomon expanded the gains made by King David through trade with the surrounding communities and nations. During his reign, Israel attained *great nation* status as he triumphed over nations acquiring treasure and property. He amassed great wealth and he had a passion for magnificence. The magnificence and splendor of his kingdom was unrivaled. Solomon was a prolific writer and his wisdom renown. "The whole world sought an audience with Solomon to hear the wisdom God had put in his heart" (1 Kings 10:24). I Kings records a great tragedy, as Solomon, who was "wiser than all men" surrendered to the temptations of wealth and women (I Kings 4: 31; 10:14-11:13). God clearly warned King Solomon not to marry women of pagan nations stating: "they'll seduce you into infatuations with their gods" (I Kings 11:2). As King Solomon's wealth, wisdom and renown proliferated, there on the mountaintop overlooking the edge, he began to lose touch of his covenant with God. Why should the foreign women who are beautiful be excluded from his kingdom which is the embodiment of beauty? What if I just marry them without consideration of their gods? How could

God declare that I have disregarded his judgments and commands if I do not worship the pagan gods? What is done in the palace has nothing to do with him, did I not build the most spectacular Temple in His honor? How could he turn away from me? Scripture states that Solomon did indeed surround himself with all the luxuries and the external grandeur of a monarch giving full sway to his sensual aspirations. According to the Bible, Solomon's reign was remarkable because of its foreign alliances. He had hundreds of wives and concubines from every nation. His wives were described as foreign princesses and included the Pharaoh's daughter, women of Moab, Ammon, Sidon and of the Hittites. These wives were instrumental in leading Solomon away from God. According to 1 Kings 11:4 Solomon's "wives turned his heart after other gods" who were their own national deities, to whom Solomon built temples. His wife Naamah, an Ammonite, was the mother of Solomon's successor, Rehoboam, who "did evil, because he prepared not his heart to seek the LORD" (II Chronicles 12:14). Jeroboam, the son of Nebat, became king of the ten tribes that revolted against the rule of Rehoboam. Solomon's kingdom was divided between Rehoboam and Jeroboam and they fought each other throughout their lives (I Kings 14:30). This was exactly the judgment that God promised to impose on Solomon for his sins of idolatry (I Kings 11:11-13). Solomon's cliffhanger experience affected his spiritual growth. Hysteria destroyed his relationship with God and any hope of a positive outcome for his future generations.

Much like the era depicted during King Solomon's reign, the world is full of riches, honors and pleasures. In search for the sensation of what manifests to our flesh as fulfillment, we pursue independence; and choosing God as an option becomes obsolete. While we bask in our freedom and separation from God we often give up our ability to make a choice. Our lives become a battleground where we are forced to fight for our lives against a disgruntled enemy, without the time to decide whether we want to or not. *The American Heritage Dictionary* defines battleground as "an area where a battle is fought or a sphere of contention."[31] The pictures in the daily news make us think that battlegrounds are places where guns are fired, bombs are exploding, people are wounded and physically killed, children are abandoned, and homes and landscapes are destroyed. Consequently, if we look around us and don't see these things happening, we think we are not living in a battlefield. Nothing could be further from the truth. Paul informs us in the second Book of Corinthians chapter 10 verses 3-5, that a spiritual battle is not like the world's physical battles. Rather, it is a battle of ideas and emotions, fought on the battlefield of the mind and heart. Henry David Thoreau affirms that as a human being: "I found in myself, and still find, an instinct toward a higher, or as it is named *spiritual* life, as do most men, and another toward a primitive, rank and savage one, and I revere them both."[32] The role of Hysteria is to present opportunities which tempt us to deny God's truth by deceiving and discouraging people so that they lose faith and hope in the goodness and providence of God. The Bible affirms that in the spiritual realm there is an evil one, Satan, who stirs up physical, emotional, philosophical, spiritual and psychological wars. These wars begin with the ideas of the mind and the passions of the heart. The cliffhanger is a call to change. We must awaken from the hysteria. Christians must follow Paul's admonition to take every thought captive until they are submissive to the will of God in Christ Jesus (2 Corinthians 10:5). Thoughts, ideas, choices and decisions must be tested by the Word of God. "For what will it profit a man if he gains the whole world, and forfeits his soul? Or what will a man give in exchange for his soul? (Matthew 16:26)

The Heart of the Christian

> *Let a man so account of us, as of the ministers of Christ, and stewards of the mysteries of God. Moreover it is required in stewards, that a man be found faithful.*
>
> I Cor. 4:1-2

The Bible emphasizes that the Christian is a sojourner on this present earth with the hope for a future utopia as God first intended. Some folk call this future place paradise, others call it heaven. The Word of God says that there will be a "new heaven and a new earth" (II Pet. 3:13). It proclaims that all things, in Him, will be new, not only in the future but upon acceptance of the gift of God in Jesus

Christ (II Cor. 5:17). This new life is the heart of the Christian. It is exemplified by a commitment to a life as a steward. A steward is defined as a person who manages another's property or financial affairs; one who administers anything as the agent of another. Words synonymous with steward include: representative, administrator, attendant, director, guardian, manager and officer. Stewardship is an ethic which entails responsible supervision of resources. A resource is more than money. It is all-inclusive consisting of time, talent, skills, abilities, knowledge, spiritual gifts and the gifts of the Spirit. Ethics represent the behavior of a collection of people to which the individual belongs. It delineates specific principles of behavior identified as a code of conduct that they are not allowed to breach. The Word of God emphasizes that, "You are not your own; you were bought at a price" (I Cor. 6:19-20). Christian stewardship invokes the image of an individual having been empowered by THE Authority to carry out functions of benefit to them both. Empowered, as the Holy Spirit reveals the truths of God, to trust and obey all of His commands. The Christian steward recognizes that specified assignments are God's assignments, and has the capacity to surrender as His servant "both to will and to work for His good pleasure" (Phil. 2:13, NIV). This is to be every Believer: a diligent, dependable manager full of the commonsense instilled by the Master and charged to feed, nurture and guide God's people at each proper time, necessitating time at the cliff's edge. In the book of Luke, chapter 12 Jesus cautions disciples not to give sway to predicaments. He encourages the Believer to know that the material things of this world are not to be our quest (Luke 12:22-31). Responsible stewardship, which applies to all God's children, entails preparation, readiness and faithfulness. Preparation involves planning with consideration of the final outcome. Readiness encompasses actively studying and comprehending the statutes of God and faithfulness is evidenced by behaviors that exhibit the importance of doing the Father's will. All illustrate the heart of a Christian; a steward who is faithful in the continuance of duty rather than submitting to the natural human proclivity for apathy, abuse and neglect (Luke 12: 45-48). A steward is required to be wise; one that is active and hopeful, offering no pretense and not displaying presumption. The Bible maintains that wise stewards are judicious for their soul. Each stint on the cliff is the time to "approach the throne of grace with confidence" (Heb. 4:16). While standing at the edge of the cliff, thoughts of evil to come, uncertainties and needless cares can cause us to avoid the call of God. The heart, which is the control center of the Christian, must overcome this fear to prevail. We have a "great High Priest who understands and sympathizes with our weaknesses" (Heb. 4:14-15). So we must exchange feelings of inadequacy and becoming discouraged for an increasingly bold faith (Eph. 3:12). As the Scriptures attest we must value our relationship with God and wait anticipatively for His return while we continue to work for His kingdom. As temporary residents, sojourners, we encounter various commentary and other obstacles regarding our faith, spirituality and standing. Jesus educates the Believer that there is a cross to bear. The Gospels state that to follow Christ and reach the goal that the Father has for us, the Believer must "take up his cross" (Mat. 10:38; 16:34; Mark 8: 34; Luke 14:27). It doesn't indicate that only some have a cross. Everyone has a cross to carry. Everyone has a cross to bear. Cross to bear means a burden or trial to face. The cross is a symbol for a heavy weight often so immobilizing that it is difficult to move forward. As noted in Scripture, persecution for being a Christian is a cross some may have to bear. Other examples of a cross may be identified as infirmity, depression, delusions, disappointments, addictions, pain, poverty, sadness, and homelessness. God says if we accept our lot and are born again, following Christ will bring unspeakable joy and all our needs will be supplied (Mat. 6:19-34; Phil. 4:19; I Pet. 1:8). Many times He does not, often by necessity, remove the cross. Still, for those who love and trust Him, "He gives strength to the weary and to him who lacks might he increases with power; those who wait for the Lord will gain new strength" (Is. 40:29, 31). The heart of the Christian is decidedly stewardship demonstrated as having knowledge and wisdom of the Word of God. Knowledge is important and having God's wisdom enables us to use this knowledge correctly. We must seek God's wisdom when faced with decisions on the mountaintop (Rom. 11:33). "The beginning of wisdom is: Acquire wisdom; and with all of your acquiring, get understanding" (Prov. 4:7). A good steward seeks the heart of God. In seeking after the heart of God, we get understanding which affects our spiritual growth.

Consider meeting someone along this journey who has reached the mountain peak. An individual caught somewhere between grief and fear; and despair makes them so angry that they lash out at everyone who comes into close proximity. You see, her mother had died a few months earlier. She had been diagnosed with a condition thought to be preventable through lifestyle changes, however, if not thwarted; it would take her life quickly. She died at an age thought by most to be too soon and now her daughter is facing the same diagnosis while dealing with the recent death of her mother. How would you feel? What would you do? She is contemptuous, hurling slurs and accusations; and growing significantly more hostile each day. God has granted you an opportunity for favor with this young lady for a time and she shares her predicament with you stating that all of the medical personnel have encouraged her to change her eating habits, food choices and exercise patterns. You tell her about God, His love in Jesus and how there are no coincidences in His design; and that perhaps the cause of her mother's illness, although not determined in time for her mom, may be the breath of life for her. She rebukes these ideas as foolish. How can eating or certain foods make you this sick? It is not that easy to instantly change the way you have been doing things for years. Why should she try when nothing helped her mom?! You continue conversing for a while. You can tell that she is at the edge of a cliff. As sick as she is, as hurt as she is over the death of her mom, as afraid as she is that her mom died with the disease she now has; can she make the ultimate choice? Can she trust and obey? Her call to change, like any child of God, has to be concise and evident. She has no time to vacillate; she has arrived at a threshold . . . the cliff's edge. Recognizing the place that she is in, you say: *I understand,* and she verbally thrashes out, ordering you to leave. You begin to leave, and as you are leaving; quietly praying for her, you realize that she has to take the next step without you being there. Her spirit is vexed and only God can help but she has to let Him. In the instance of acknowledging God's specific assignment, questioning one's ability is natural. You are burdened with the thought of failure. Then it becomes evident that you must *deny yourself and take up your cross.* This is yielding. Yielding is an act of the will. She was not ready, yet. The road ahead frightened her and she believed she would have to travel it alone. Unfortunately, she surmised that she had always been alone. Although her spiritual growth was within reach, she was unable to grasp its reality.

In the Book of Acts we are informed of a Christian named Stephen who was appointed as an overseer to care for the widows. Stephen is described as one full of the Holy Spirit with wisdom and faith who had accomplished many great wonders and signs (Acts 6: 5-6, 8). Acts 7:55, states that Stephen exceeded many in the performance of his duties. "Some men from the Synagogue of the Freedmen, *including* Cyrenians and Alexandrians, and some from Cilicia and Asia, argued with Stephen. But they were unable to cope with the wisdom and the Spirit with which he *spoke*" (Acts 6: 9-10). As a result of his newfound allegiance to Christianity, Stephen engaged in disputations with these unconverted peoples and it is inferred that he was arrested at their instigation. Brought before the Sanhedrin as a blasphemer and an apostate, he endeavored to prove that the presence and favor of God is not confined; and the same ungrateful, disparaging and depraved spirit that has always been portrayed since receiving their freedom by God was still evident. Stephen observed a change in the affect of his judges and was intuitively alerted to the probability that the end of his physical life was near. As a good steward, he was compelled to teach, addressing the limitlessness of God; and there in front of a mass crowd of the unbelieving he had to decide his fate. Should he confront the customs and traditions which were in opposition to the love God proposed in Christ? Will the crowd allow him to quantify history and hear the truths regarding Jesus, in the narratives of Abraham, Jacob, Joseph, Moses, David and the prophets? How could he, one who has accepted Jesus as Messiah, speak about the coming judgment of God on Israel, Jerusalem and the temple? How does a steward prepare for such service? When our will is opposite the Lord's will, we must choose His. Stephen had demonstrated an exacting will in his disputes over injustice, limiting God's grace and the ensuing new covenant. However, even with his fateful experience at the edge of the cliff and knowledge of his ensuing fatality, there was the revelation of a loving and gracious Spirit-filled being. He presented as a man with compassion; a diligent and dependable manager. This wise steward stood falsely accused, yet fervent in ardor and mighty in power presented an impassioned message. Although this led to his death, his decision at the cliff influenced his spiritual development and the spiritual maturity of many others. This moment has received special emphasis in the teachings of God's Word and Stephen is distinguished as the first Christian martyr.

When thou passest through the waters I will be with thee,
and through the rivers, they shall not overflow thee.

(Isaiah 43:2, KJV)

Chapter Seven

Conclusion

The early churches were called Believers and each Believer was called a saint because of their faith. The word saint means sanctified or set apart to God. It is used most frequently in Paul's Epistles and denotes a universal designation for all Christians. Faith in God through Jesus Christ is the essence of the Believer. Mankind's expressed relationship with God is the "blending of fear and trust" which is evident as faith.[33] Christ is the Author and Finisher of our faith (Heb. 12:2). For Christians the essential idea is that we become holy or set apart in character as exemplified by our faith in Jesus. We are a saint because of faith. A relationship is confirmed in our faith and at the edge of the cliff of decision, faith is on trial. Whether a Believer or a nonbeliever, faith in the existence of God, the reality of His personal involvement in our lives, the promises espoused as biblical truth and the contractual agreement for an inextinguishable life enacted through belief in the sacrificial death of Jesus are tested in the cliffhanger experience. "Good judgment wins favor, but the way of the unfaithful leads to destruction" (Prov. 13:16). So, although granted the ability to choose, our choices do not alter the consequences of our choices.

There was a blind man named Bartimaeus who was persistent in faith. He was sitting alongside of the road which Jesus travelled and hearing much clamoring, inquired as to the reason for such commotion. After being told that Jesus of Nazareth was passing by;

he called out, saying, "Jesus, Son of David, have mercy on me!" (Luke 18: 37-38). Jesus' disciples considered Bartimaeus to be beneath Jesus' notice. Bartimaeus persisted in calling out to Jesus for help, despite the people who attempted to silence him. He had faith that Jesus could correct his eyesight. Jesus stopped and said, "Call him *here*." So the disciples called the blind man, saying to him, "Take courage, stand up, He is calling for you;" and throwing aside his cloak, Bartimaeus jumped up and went to Jesus. (Mark 10:49-50). The Bible states that faith begins when God speaks (Rom 10:17). Bartimaeus exercised his faith by responding to what God told him to do. Jesus replied, "Go; your faith has made you well." (Mark 10:52). The people witnessing the man take steps toward the unfamiliar for restoration; trusting God in the dark and jumping of the cliff into what appeared to be nothing and nowhere, affirmed the miracle by praising God. Following his healing, Bartimaeus followed Jesus remaining steadfast after his experience of leaving his mountain cliff. Persistence, anticipation, faith and gratitude are the conclusion of a cliff experience firmly fixed in the will of God. First John 5:14 asks, "Do we have the faith to receive what is the will of God for us?" Dr. David Jeremiah, in his daily devotional attests that to *walk by faith and not by sight* seems contrary to commonsense. It means that we "only have God's promises with which to face an uncertain future."[34] The basis of human nature is to require tangible evidence for faith such as cash-in hand, "buildings, traditions, rituals, schedules, liturgies, ministers and the like" to have something to "pin our hopes on."[35] Through faith we avail ourselves of miracles, wonders, testimony and historical evidence that God has kept His promises to those who trust Him and believe that He will keep us. God keeps His promises, but He has not promised to support eccentricities, whims and fancies. Faith is not blind. It is not predicated upon illusion, deception or wishful thinking. Its basis and foundation is on the inseparable link between God and mankind. That inseparable link is called GRACE. It is grace found in Jesus, given to the undeserving. We accept this grace by faith "and God is able to make all grace abound toward us, the saints of God; that we **always**, having **all** sufficiency in **all** things, may abound to **every** good work" (II Cor. 9:8). The framework, value and fuel of our spiritual existence reside at each pinnacle of our mountaintop experiences.

First John 5:4 says "for whosoever is born of God overcomes the world: and this is the victory that overcomes the world, even our faith." Victory is that inner peace of God which "surpasses all understanding" (Phil. 4:7). It is the joy of the Lord which is our strength (Neh. 8:10). It is the inner confidence that overcomes discouragement, doubt and unbelief. It is the assurance that God is in control of "them who are the called according to His purpose," and as we love the Lord and live a life wholly consecrated to Him, we know all things and circumstances are somehow working "together for our good" (Rom. 8:28). A victorious life of faith is not one that is lived by methodologies, sentiments or circumstances. As often as many of us try, faith cannot be manipulated by our mind, will or emotions. As Believers, we are to live and abide according to what the Word of God says, not according to our situations or traditions of men; "We walk by faith and not by sight" (II Cor. 5:7). This walk of faith is what brings victory. The leap of faith required at the cliff's edge may not be sanctioned to change some external circumstance in your life. Instead, God may be calling for a decision within your circumstances, to challenge tradition that opposes the intent of His Word or to change YOU internally. Our times on the cliff are in direct correlation to challenge where our spiritual growth ensues and we come to understand that challenging situations are often on behalf of Christ; having Him in view for honor, as "it has been granted for Christ's sake, not only to believe in Him, but also to suffer for His sake" (Phil. 1:29). Our faith means we believe that in spite of appearances, the Lord will change conditions but in the meantime, faith provides that we can find peace and refuge by remaining in His presence. This is God's promised "way of escape;" that in the midst of discomfort abiding in Him shall give us peace, in the midst of conflict there shall be victory and in the midst of turmoil we shall have tranquility (1 Corinthians 10:13). The acknowledged presence of God enables us to have victory in our life. Victory does not take intellect, philosophy or strategy. To be the victor over your mountain crest moments, simply put, it takes faith. Faith will take you over, in and through your dilemma. It can be exemplified in every distressing situation (Heb. 11:32-42). According to the Book of Hebrews, chapter 11 faith is perseverance which leads to deliverance whereby God is glorified. Faith will often ease the effects of an incident though it will not alter the circumstances. The transforming power of faith is a deliberate process. Paul's conversion and resultant faith wrought an unrelenting change in his attitude. At first being adversarial to the cause of Christ, his contention became to "press toward the mark for the prize of the high calling of God in Christ Jesus" (Phil. 4:13). His cliff experience produced a transformation that took him from a place of absolute opposition to a place of total surrender, the place that every Believer must arrive and of this we should never lose sight; for surrender affords the capacity for spiritual attainment, maturation and victory far beyond human possibilities.

Cliffhangers present the individual with possibilities. The possibilities insinuate that there are choices and that there are decisions to be made. We have all seen the picture of the footprints in the sand and read the short story of how God carried the individual during the hardest times in life thus the explanation for only one set of footprints. This rendering always evokes the heart of a Christian as one reflects on the grace and mercy of God. Grace and mercy is used by God to reprove pride, vanity and self-sufficiency. His grace is bestowed without regard to worth, merit or what the individual deserves. Grace gives impetus to faith which allows the Holy Spirit to exert His influence on the soul of man, turns him toward Christ, delivers, keeps and strengthens his faith and creates a deep and abiding relationship with God. Footprints in the sand deliver the message of mercy as our accompanying thoughts remind us of our fallibility, helplessness and hopelessness; and requisite need of a savior. It conjures up reflections of our hopes and knowing that God keeps His promises, how He is always with us and always here for us even when we doubt. It reminds us that His "grace is *indeed* sufficient and His mercy is everlasting" (I Cor. 12:9; Ps. 100:5, KJV). Like the narrative, mercy offers comfort (II Cor. l 1:3-4). God's demonstration of His love for mankind is by His mercy (Eph.2:4). But most fail to affirm that the portrayal of footprints in the sand and its narrative also symbolizes our surrender and God's control. The glory of the world is worthless. Piety and usefulness are the products of surrender and is to be valued. The cliffhanger is God's design to humble us and bring us to repentance. Many walk contrary to this in disbelief.

This unbelief produces contempt of God and a willful abandonment of spiritual development. God does not impose His will. We must choose His will. Standing there on your cliff one is challenged to give all control to God, to abandon the self and live for Him. You stand there on the cliff vacillating between possibilities. There is a threshold of faith for everyone that God has permitted during this earthly existence. Each cliffhanger is an example of God allowing us to experience His perfect work of taking us from one realm of spiritual development to another. The Scriptures propose many narratives on the importance of our attitude of faith toward God, while the world offers a myriad of possibilities; but only surrender inculcates the spiritual development sanctioned in the Word of God. Each instance at the cliff's edge demonstrates that a moment of decision influences spiritual consciousness. The cliffhanger is unique for each individual although its aim to effect spiritual growth is the same. Each person's mountain climb is unique and each decision is important for their spiritual wellbeing. Every decision leads to somewhere even when no choice is made. It is a fact of life that even a dead-end road is still considered somewhere. While some paths may lead to positive outcomes others may lead to sorrow, regret or death. Facing life and its challenges, individuals pursue a perceived idea of life and standing on the edge, experience on the cliff presents a time of discovery. Each venture is a lesson concerning how we participate in God's purpose and how our faith is expressed through our life events and relationships. The biblical expectation of the Believer is to embody the great commission of our Lord. This is to be the agenda of every Christian. However, it is often at odds with the dominant societal and cultural values and many times with our local churches. The pursuit of wealth, status, comfort and the promotion of our own agenda, rather than God's agenda are conflicting issues within the Kingdom of God. What we value is demonstrated by our commitment which is often forgotten at the many peaks of decision. Value refers to the relative worth or quality of an object. Value is what makes something desirable or undesirable. Values, therefore, influences one's behavior. What we value guides personal choices. The Bible contends that "where the treasure is; the heart is also" (Mat. 6:21). We are required to be committed to God and each other with attention on His Kingdom building because of the mercy and grace demonstrated in and through Jesus. As we climb the many mountains in life, we must explore the difficult questions regarding its implications, address the struggles, support one another and attempt to remain steadfast until God's purposes are revealed. This will elicit spiritual growth and a bona fide relationship in Christ.

Spiritual growth can come through unpopular choices. Every choice we make throughout the years impacts the person we will become. Along the mountain trail, the good and bad decisions we will make at each cliff are all known by God. It is written that temptation to compromise and commit immorality is common to humankind (Mat. 26: 41; Gal. 5:19-21). But, if we trust God and recognize that all temptation occurs on a spiritual level, and grow in relationship with Him; we have discovered the means of "escape" (I Cor. 10:13). Just as Jesus commanded the removal of grave clothes from Lazarus that held him bound, the Lord has removed all evidences of bondage from the Believer, yet still has to ask "where is your faith?'(Luke 5:25). Poised upon the crag of a mountain you look for signs of life, for a bottom or something to hold onto that will help you descend. But there is nothing. *Where is your faith?* You cannot climb down, there is no magic carpet and you have no wings. You imagine no support and no help. How did you get here? How will you stay alive if all there is left to do is jump? This is an unpopular choice. Some stay in this place a long time. Some never leave. They watch the days and nights, the seasons and years as they come and go. Sometimes the storms are hard and they are weather beaten, but they stay still; afraid to leave—afraid to jump. *Where is your faith?* Many individuals are not risk-takers, especially when it is related to things of God. Individuals who are not risk-takers are described as conservative and conventional in the ways they live. They often play it safe, choosing the *tried-and-true* method in every situation. In most instances this strategy appears to work to their advantage. Some people are afraid of taking the risk to possibly fail, some are afraid to give up what they believe is *having control*; while others rely on waiting for things to happen. Waiting on things to happen is often determined by various cultures to be passive. But, having faith in God and allowing Him to lead is not passivity. To some people the conservative approach portrays a lack of trust and confidence in the Lord. The Bible provides evidence of multiple individuals waiting on God and others stepping out on faith. We have been created by God as uniquely His children. We choose to be active predicated upon an innate God-given capacity, initiative, and life experiences to make choices and exercise creativity. The experience of being active means attending to the business of growing spiritually which involves consistent responsiveness, faithfulness and effort. The Word of God affirms that, "this race is not to the swift, nor the battle to the strong…time and chance happen to them all" (Eccles. 9:11, ESV). Instead of allowing circumstances to take advantage or to accept them fatalistically, we all have to fight to challenge the status quo; the wiles of the evil one which is akin to bondage (Eph. 6:11). Faith is the way to enter into the grace of God enabling God to lead through unpopular choices (Rom. 5:2). Therefore, if God is permitted to lead in all circumstances, the Believer is liberated from the burden of the outcome. When we trust in Him, we're free to say whatever needs to be said, bold enough to go wherever we need to go and confident to do what has to be done. As spiritual growth allows us to attain "a glorious inner strength," the mountain adventure and ultimate cliff allows each Believer to "reach out and experience the breadth! Test its length! Plunge the depths! Rise to the heights! And live full lives! Full in the fullness of God" (Eph. 3:11-19, The Message). Unpopular lives…unpopular choices… can lead you to God.

"Be holy, for I am holy" is the command of God (I Pet. 1:16, NKJ). "This is the will of God, your sanctification." (1 Thessalonians 4:3). No one experiences this sanctification without death of the old self before repentance and acceptance of the grace of God in Jesus Christ. If this crucial moment of change has never occurred then sanctification will forever be an elusive hope. One purpose of theology in history has been to challenge and change insidiousness, mal-practices, defective ideologies and often misguided assumptions about the world of Christianity, its people, and its Creator. According to the Word of God, if this means that a breach is required between father and son, mother and daughter, then God, because He reserves sole authority will allow this to happen. There are no agendas, hidden or otherwise, it is all about God and the work of His Kingdom. God who offers no consideration for rank, position, ethnicity or gender orchestrates the life of every individual for the fulfillment of His plan. God's ways are neither man's ways nor His thoughts like man's thoughts (Is. 55:8). He is the true God and only He can reveal events before they come to pass always having his purpose in view (Is.

45:8-11). He is not complacent regarding the affairs of humankind. "He chose us before the foundation of the world that we should be holy and without blame before Him. In love, He predestined us for adoption through Jesus Christ to Himself, according to the kind intentions of His will" (Eph. 1:4-5). Cyrus, King of Persia, was a Gentile who, as it is written in the Old Testament, received God's anointing. Exhibiting His omniscience, God had declared this to Isaiah hundreds of years prior to the birth of Cyrus (Is. 44:28):

> Thus says the LORD, your Redeemer, and the one who formed you from the womb, I, the LORD, am the maker of all things, Stretching out the heavens by Myself And spreading out the earth all alone, Causing the omens of boasters to fail, Making fools out of diviners, Causing wise men to draw back And turning their knowledge into foolishness, Confirming the word of His servant And performing the purpose of His messengers. It is I who says of Jerusalem, 'She shall be inhabited!' And of the cities of Judah, 'They shall be built.' And I will raise up her ruins again. It is I who says to the depth of the sea, 'Be dried up!' And I will make your rivers dry. It is I who says of Cyrus, 'He is My shepherd! And he will perform all My desire.' And he declares of Jerusalem, She will be built, And of the temple, Your foundation will be laid. Isaiah 44:24-28

Being a Gentile indicates that he had no prior acknowledgment of Israel's God. Cyrus was a renowned military victor. The history of these victories during ancient times reveals the belief that conquests in battle were attributed to the conqueror's god. Nations were terrified upon hearing of Cyrus' advance and they erected idols to save themselves. The cliffhanger Cyrus would experience required him to choose a covenantal relationship with the One, True God or be comforted by his own humanity with its emphasis on self-righteousness and self-worship. The Bible contends that God called Cyrus specifically by name for a task, proved His existence and offered Cyrus strength in battle, riches and honor (Is. 45:1-8). Did the most powerful God of Israel really call him, a Gentile, by name? Could the Lord really expect Cyrus to intervene on behalf of

Israel? Babylon is such a great nation, why should he get involved? Cyrus recognized and regarded the call of God. He acknowledged God as the One who always guided and empowered him (Ezra 1:2). Cyrus proved that faith is not just a statement of belief. It is dynamic, evolving and relational. It shapes the way we see things and how we construct our life's meaning. Faith exerts restraint or direction over our values and perceptions. It is evident in our conceptualization of power. Being tied closely to self-image and worldview, one's perception of self and the world are influenced by faith. It is a complex social, psychological and spiritual phenomenon. God through His Holy Spirit wants to strengthen faith and to make it more mature. As faith matures it represents holiness. Experiences at the edge of mountaintops stimulate the establishment or growth of faith. Under God's anointing Cyrus had been assured of God's presence, help, love and care. His faith confirmed a relationship with sustaining power to carry him through whatever the assignment to be performed. God empowered Cyrus and he conquered Babylon. But, he had to leave the comfort of his mountaintop first. He delivered an exiled Israel, recovered articles of worship and paved the way toward the rebuilding of the Temple. If we continue in faith, stable and steadfast to "walk in a manner worthy of the Lord, fully pleasing to Him, bearing fruit in every good work and increasing in the knowledge of God" prevailing over the cliff is not an option (Col. 1:9-12). The Bible resolves that Jesus must have supremacy over the life of the Believer which is displayed through faith; then Christians are presented as blameless, above reproach and holy. As we journey through the mountain reaching each cliff's edge, every excursion is a route where restoration and transformation develops the Believer's depth of understanding and spirituality.

While the lady mountaineers embarked on their mountain journey they endured much. Upon their return they disclosed that there were many trials, tribulations, joys and sorrows. Out of seemingly tragic circumstances came blessings. We can never know the value of any experience during the time of experiencing it. It is inconceivable to comprehend whether that which brings much anguish will be a blessing in the future. The Word of God states that "the man who endures trials is blessed, for when he has stood the test, he will receive the crown of life which God has promised to those who love Him" (James 1:12). Tests, trials, difficult and unpopular choices, unforeseen circumstances and hard decisions, when seen through the lens of faith become opportunities to cooperate with God. The passage of time following the moment of decision is the only way to ascertain the true worth of an experience. Oftentimes choices bring consequences that have a profound effect on the life of an individual leading to suffering and according to Scriptures, faith brings victory over suffering (Rom. 8:18-25). The Book of James reminds us that because of our limitations as human beings, we don't have the capacity to know and judge the true value of any situation in life. Instances in life can have positive or negative value. Things perceived by the natural mind as positive may render negative results while those perceived as negative can manifest positive value. Sometimes, we may be able to discern the value of an incident; this is especially the time that we must become skilled at focusing our faith, believing God is always working to bring good to His children (Luke 11:13). But we must take care that in all of our expecting through faith that wisdom is not discounted. Standing on the mountain of decision we must pray for wisdom to see our situation from God's perspective. Much like the issues faced by the female mountaineers, there are times that Believers come face to face with apparently insurmountable mountain journeys and ostensibly we are dangling at the end of a rope at the limit of all endurance. Travelling along the paths of life perceiving them only as an adventure is not an option for the Believer as it was for the female mountaineers. There atop the mountain cliff the only choices may be to wait and do nothing or to not decide anything at all. Sometimes these are the choices to be made and other times it is necessary to act. Sometimes, just like the early mountaineers, we find ourselves "lured and beckoned" by the quest of the next hill that causes us to become distracted which can bring mistakes causing injury or death.[36] It is often during these times of losing our way or stumbling along the trail that we examine our faith or we question our calling. Our faith is not limited to one aspect of our lives. It does not stop at our salvation experience. It is not merely a religious practice or observance. Our faith is to become all-encompassing as it illustrates our Christian walk being rooted in God's Truth. Much like the lady mountaineers, "it will give us a strong body, controlled nerves, poise and a calmness of mind . . .

It will arouse the adventurous, exploring spirit . . . It will result in a growth and a development of your spiritual and mental being."[37] The perspective of the cliffhanger experience as a trial of faith in God enables spiritual growth. This view will undoubtedly cause one to discard much of the pettiness in this life providing a futuristic outlook of eternal proportions which may aid the Believer to live up to the conditions and possibilities of the new life that God has planned. T. D. Jakes writes in *Peaks and Valleys* that "great growth comes through the valleys and low places where you feel limited and vulnerable."[38] I concur that during these times we seek the solace and guidance of God but I contend that the experience on the mountain peak where no other surface can be seen is a time where the rubber meets the road; where your faith and character are tested. It is true that obedience can be acquired through afflictions in the valley. Sometimes we must wait there in the valley for God to deliver us although He may still sustain us. Sometimes the waiting causes affliction. Obedience learned during affliction is summoned at the cliff; it is here where the effect of spiritual growth is demonstrated. Standing at the edge of the cliff you must determine to stay there or jump. There are no alternatives, no other rest stops or places for nurture. Since you can no longer climb, descent necessitates a choice. God has brought you this far. You have arrived at the end of a cycle in life. Like traveling on a train that has reached its destination, do you ride on or get off here?

JUDGE NOT

Judge not; the workings of the brain
And of the heart thou can'st not see;
What looks to thy dim eye a stain,
In God's pure light may only be
A scar, brought from some well-won field,
Where thou would'st only faint and yield.

The look, the air, that frets thy sight,
May be a token that below
The soul had closed in deadly fight
With some internal, fiery foe,
Whose glance would scorch thy smiling grace,
And cast thee, shuddering, on thy face.

The fall thou darest to despise:
May be the angel's slackened hand
Has suffered it that he may rise
And take a firmer, surer stand;
Or, trusting less to earthly things,
May henceforth learn to use his wings.

And judge none lost; but wait and see,
With hopeful pity, not disdain;
The depth of the abyss may be
The measure of the height of pain
And love and glory that may raise
This soul to God in after days.

Adelaide Proctor.

APPENDIX A

What shall we do with Jesus?

In Matthew 27:11-22, we read of Jesus standing before Pontius Pilate, the Roman Governor, awaiting indictment. While Jesus did not dispel the accusation of being King of the Jews; He refused to defend Himself against the accusations of blasphemy by the chief priests and elders. His silence amazed Pilate who sought to release Jesus, but the multitude asked for Barabbas instead, which prompted Pilate to ask the question: "What, then, shall I do with Jesus who is called Christ" (Mat. 27:22)? Our Spiritual Growth Journey answers this question and the answers allow us to see where we are along the mountain. It also can provide a glimpse into the reason for a Believer's choices at the cliff. Biblical accounts can teach and comfort us in many spiritual and natural situations. It is important to realize that there can be no natural augmentation without spiritual association. One does not distinctly negate one over the other. This is why the Bible says that "the Word of God," which "is alive and active *and* sharper than any double-edged sword, penetrates even to dividing soul and spirit" (Heb.4:12). The Word of God is keenly accurate and allows the one who searches its Truths to see their natural soul and spirit, individually and collectively. Then, the redemptive message of the Gospel can lead them to Jesus as the living example of how God wants us to live in Him and who God wants us to be. The natural and the spiritual are entangled, illustrated by the statement, "so as he thinks in himself, so he is" (Prov. 23:7). An outward veneer of

Christianity is only momentary as the tremendous struggles involved exact formidable pressure. The Holy Spirit confirms, convicts, and attempts to change a person. The message of the Bible informs us that "it judges the thoughts and attitudes of the heart; and nothing in all creation is hidden from God's sight. Everything is uncovered and lay bare before the eyes of Him to whom we must give account" (Heb.4:12-13). This knowledge must be powered by faith. It is most important to conclude with the fact that unbelief and rebellion keeps individuals out of God's inheritance. *What do we do with Jesus?* Do we believe that He is who He said He is? Every cliff experience involves decisive actions and the outcomes are not based on good or bad luck. The cliffhanger's disposition is to influence spiritual knowledge and understanding about life; YOUR LIFE. The very life that existed entombed in a suspension, arrived gasping for breath and as the myriad of evils assail, has had to vie earnestly for longevity; whether it has been unfaithful friends, lost loved ones, impromptu liaisons or shady business deals; not to mention murders, burglaries, incest, rape and the list is unending. Ask yourself, how could you come to be here by chance? Would you have deliberately initiated the problems of your life? God's Word reinforces the need to be taught and have the Good News preached to the unbelieving, but to be beneficial spiritually and naturally, one must have this knowledge "mixed with faith" (Heb. 4:2, NKJV). The question must be answered: *What do I do with Jesus the Christ?* Do I believe, accept Him as my example for living, hide Him on a shelf or reveal Him only when I need to? The temptation to merely profess Jesus and then renounce Him by our behaviors must be resisted.

The word for spiritual in the New Testament is the Greek word pneumatikis. It is translated from Hebrew as ruach meaning breath or wind. Jesus informed Nicodemus, a religious leader, that, "unless one is born of water and the Spirit he cannot enter into the kingdom of God. That which is born of the flesh is flesh, and that which is born of the Spirit is spirit" (John 3:5-7). In these uses of the word, "spirit" within biblical context it is obvious that the Holy Spirit plays a significant role in the Believer's spirituality. The Spirit is sent as a comforter, guide, and to "expose the error of the godless world's view of sin, righteousness, and judgment" (John 16:7-8, 13, Msg). When Christians are motivated and expressly made active through the power of the Holy Spirit they may be regarded as spiritual. It is a fundamental quality whereby the Believer's identity is determined by their association in Christ (Gal. 2:20). The outcome of this association is recognition that, "Surely you too are *one* of them; for even the way you talk gives you away" (Mat. 26:73). According to the Scriptures, being spiritual means being aware of Jesus' role as the crucified and risen savior enabling faith to abound and allowing the wisdom of God to pervade the life of the Christian resulting in a deeper understanding of God's plan. Spirituality is exemplified by each person at various levels or stages of spiritual maturity. Much like Erik Erikson's psychological analysis of the psychosocial development of humanity, spiritual growth can be organized as stages in life. None of these stages or levels has any bearing on salvation. Salvation is received upon faithful acceptance of God's grace with repentance. However, there is an indication that varying degrees of knowledge and faith affect an individual's choices on the cliff, therefore impacting spiritual maturity. The foundation of Erikson's philosophy is deemed by many scholars to have two major premises: that the world grows bigger and more complex as we experience life's stages and failure in life is cumulative. Whether in agreement or not the consensus among scholars is that the strength of the human spirit can overcome insufficiency. As Erikson articulated eight stages through which a healthily developing human should pass from infancy to adulthood, there are comparable stages of spiritual development which will be called the Stairway of Spiritual Life. In each stage there are challenges the person must confront and hopefully master. Each stage builds on the successful completion of an earlier stage. Often a Christian remains in a specific stage for many years. This may be due to shame, doubt, confusion, and poor self-esteem, limited faith, isolation, wrong choices or indecisions. It can be surmised that much like Erikson's theory of psychosocial development, the challenges of the stages of spiritual development not successfully managed, may be expected to reappear as future problems for the Believer.

The following chart provides the classification of characteristics of each of 9 distinct stages in the spiritual growth cycle. These diagram and descriptions are an analysis of displayed characteristics that may be indicative of spiritual maturation, rather than its conclusion. As you peruse the information provided, it may be determined that there is an overlap and you may see yourself between stages. This is highly probable. Consideration must be given to the cognitive nature of this concept. Stages are rarely skipped, though as mention many find themselves between two. Progress through the stages is successive; however, individuals progress at different rates. It is extremely rare to regress backward in stages. Each stage toward spiritual maturity provides a new and necessary perspective, more comprehension, and more awareness of life's complexities and of the finality of the physical world. Spiritual development is not the result of reasoning but of faith, knowledge and wisdom which comes from God under the auspices of each cliff experience.

STAIRWAY OF SPIRITUAL LIFE

Based on Erikson's Model

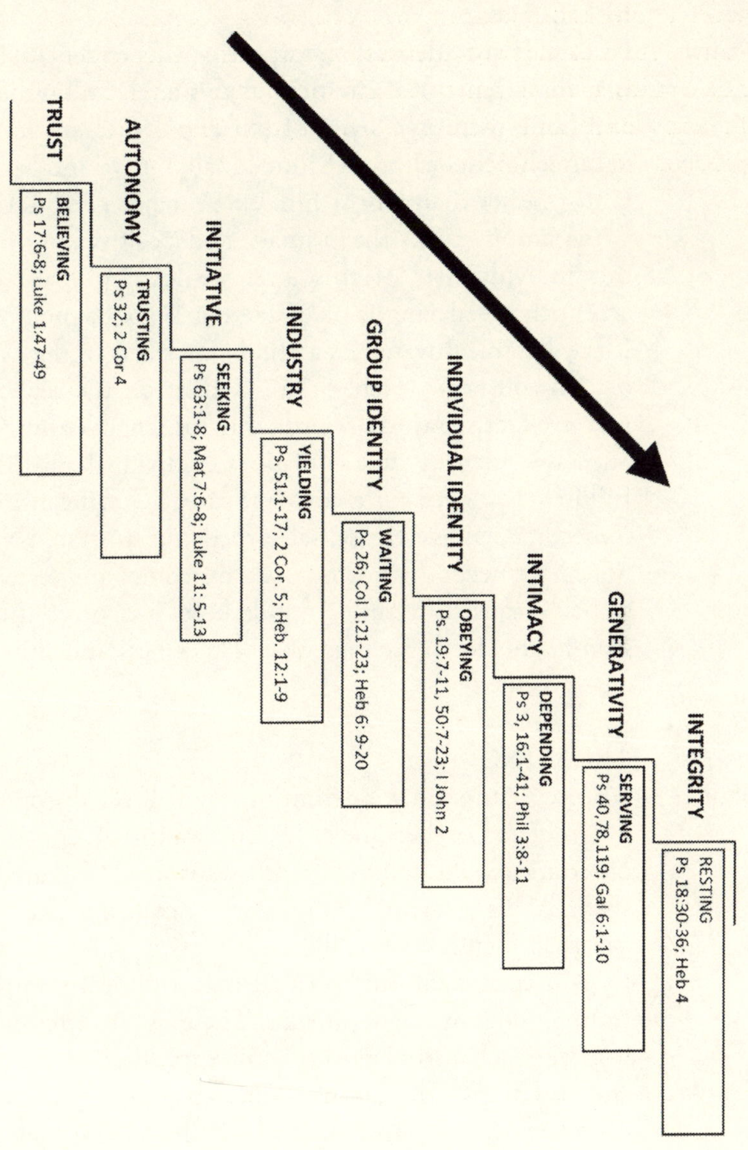

STAIRWAY OF SPIRITUAL LIFE

Description

Stage 1 BELIEVING

Stair I Feature: Trust (definition: expecting, dependent) There is a "new" sense of excitement at this level. Full of desire and hope there is a sense of self and a primary feeling of attachment with the individual(s) that introduced Christ rather than Christ himself. A major need noticed is the emphasis on the primary and positive care from this individual(s). At this level we learn to trust and accept that believing is okay. Here it is about me, mine, I feel, I think, I want: As a child "unskilled in the Word of righteousness" (Heb. 5:13). Reliant on the senses to perceive God; prayers are primarily for tangible things.

Success= Identity as a distinct individual in Him. Failure= The need for a constant caregiver can cause one to become narcissistic, self-absorbed and frustrated when hoped for needs are not met. All outcomes are perceived as being caused by the self and the desire for control is seen at this level; feelings of worthlessness and mistrust are developed

Stage 2 TRUSTING

Stair II Feature: Autonomy (definition: self-directed; on my own) Here we become a distinct spiritual entity full of courage and self-will; and want to be treated as such: "This is who I am, now!" Acquiring skills for spiritual identity i.e. Bible reading/studying, we seek to gain control of our spiritual maturity; learning right from wrong by own pursuit. There is an attempt to live by one's own law, but still expecting, dependent and needing affirmation. Vulnerable to "every wind of doctrine; relationships with Believers and familiar unbelievers are impactful. Previous actions do not

bring about the same results; learning that one must change own behavior to change responses. A time of exploration: learning about the *new* self and abilities.
Success= Developed capabilities, outgoing, confident in knowing God through Christ
Failure= if doubt or shame emerges can become inhibited and secretive

Stage 3 SEEKING
Stair III Feature: Initiative (Definition: ingenuity, set into motion)
Humility must be developed and disappointment curtailed. There is a need to be unpretentious as the "new" self will be challenged by external concerns, competencies, learned skills and the need for management of the many situations encountered on this spiritual growth journey. Repentant and full of purpose we aspire to copy those we respect within our spiritual circles causing appraisal and testing in situations often with difficulty pulling away when conflicting. Here, follow the leader, role play and attempting to make the Scriptures fit one's own perspective may be evident.
Success= Prepared to cope with potential difficulties and controversies to values, principles, beliefs, etc. A love for God manifests.
Failure= Self-doubt, inner conflict, depression, or remorseful acceptance; guilt over what is in the past and unstable alliance

Stage 4 YIELDING
Stair IV Feature: Industry (Definition: diligence, accomplishment)
Spiritual independence and risky behavior are the characteristics of this stage. Full of ideas and competence you find it necessary to step outside of the familiar and learn how to function yet, still requiring the provision of spiritual food through others. The growth process toward spiritual maturation is measured by what the Bible says as we have a better understanding of our own beliefs. Peer learning is noted at this level; having similar values

and interests, peers become validation of self. Care must be taken here because we are in an unfavorable position of becoming judgmental; even a promoter of one's own spiritual capacities.

Success= Spirit-led, a controlled self-will and upwardly challenged

Failure= Helter-Skelter, No focus, indecisive; may experience unresolved feelings of inadequacy and inferiority among peers

Stage 5 WAITING

Stair V Group Identity

Feature: Distinctive (Definition: unique; exceptional) We move outside the immediate to a larger community; which presents transitional challenges and phases of preparation such as choices regarding religious paths of influence; uncertainty regarding calling and goals; Full of devotion, there is a penchant for the ideal which is conflict-free versus reality with its conflict. Community and familial relationships are significant to spiritual growth. Here you identify models of spiritual competency, prestige, popularity; often seeking affirmation and motivation. This is the spiritual level where there is an increased potential for adverse relationships that can adversely affect your growth. May lead to a withdrawal from previous responsibilities during your searching for who you are in Him; **Beware!** less you become vulnerable to stress, hampered by spiritual priorities and role confusion Success= Developing skills and capabilities which enable the Holy Spirit's management of one's motivation, emotional states and thought processes Failure= Unwillingness to discard old belief system "having a form of godliness' (1 Tim 3:4-6)

Stage 6 OBEYING

Stair VI Individual Identity

Feature: Association (Definition: Connection; Communion) *It is one thing to get started, and yet another to do well and advance in it.* This stage characterizes experimentation. Full of fidelity you recognize spiritual gifting or calling and make strides toward God's commission. Your relationship with God has increased; there is a belief in one-self and who you are spiritually: aspirations, level of interests, activities and accomplishment tend toward spirituality. You have become separate and distinct, "walking with God." At this level one assumes responsibility for gaining knowledge and deepening one's relationship with God. You learn to prioritize your spiritual life against all other facets of life. Having this higher sense of self-regulation, you attempt to not let outside forces dictate your actions any longer. Your *walk* with God becomes a personal investment. You are steadfast; resilient, walk by faith and more often able to effectively cope with "setbacks" and "let downs."

Success= Strengthened relationship with God and Believers; better able to navigate life's disturbances and discord. Ministerial (service) interests are developed. Successful navigation of this stage brings intimacy with God on a deeper level.

Failure= Contented isolation; Spirituality is seen as purely personal venture; you may become self-seeking; we can feel superior to others and become segregated

Stage 7 DEPENDING

Stair VII Feature: Intimacy (Definition: comfortable, familiar and free) Here there is the need to manage interdependent relationships such as family, social, community, work, educational, recreational, physical, etc. allowing the inclusion necessary for the spiritual development of others while assuring that your basic spiritual needs are met and protected. You demonstrate an interest in creativity and meaningful issues encompassing family and friend:. "Do you know my Jesus?" Most likely you have acquired keen spiritual discernment; "the mature . . . those who have their powers of discernment trained by constant practice to distinguish good from evil" (Heb. 5:14). The level of commitment required at this level is total . . . full of love and affiliation. You are becoming physically, intellectually and emotionally secure in Him; becoming secure in your walk and spiritual development of mind, body, will and emotions. We are commanded to love God with all our heart, all our mind, and with all our soul (Matthew 22:37). At this level, we seek to love others the same.

Success= Security and comfort; unspeakable joy; peace like a river; an unquenchable desire to pass it on Failure= Displaced Christian; displays of carnality; worldliness; Isolation

Stage 8 SERVING

Stair VIII Feature: Generativity* (Definition: a need to nurture, guide and contribute to the next generation) This can be expressed in many ways, from raising children, changing culture and tradition, to restoring society. Seeking fulfillment you are full of meaning and purpose. You try to *make a difference* with your life, to *give back*, to *take care* of your community and your planet. Christian life has become an established routine. Many begin to feel their spiritual footing is shaken when life becomes somewhat static. Inactivity and meaninglessness are disconcerting, as there is a need to be fruitful for God. Adjustment is required and one begins the performance of self-reappraisals in which one considers abilities to assist the next generation in their spiritual walk. Paul says "I have become all things to all people that by all means I might save some," (1 Cor. 9:22);

Success= Adaptable, God-centered, driven to fulfill purpose and find meanings; extension outside into the community

---

* Generativity: A term coined by the psychoanalyst Erik Erikson to denote the strength that comes from the care of others and production of something that contributes to the betterment of society.

Failure= inability to advance toward the fulfillment of God's directive for one's life, can get lost in constantly making comparisons to others you consider more adept and time is wasted identifying complications. Other people, especially *the unsaved* are seen as challenges to religious lifestyle; a return to self-centric behaviors; haughtiness "they brought it on themselves;" Stagnation

Stage 9 RESTING

Stair IX Feature: Integrity (Definition: The state of being whole, steadfast) Perception of relationship with God is most important at this stage. Full of wisdom; identified as reliability and trust in Him. "For I know whom I have believed, and I am convinced that he is able to guard until that day what has been entrusted to me" (2 Tim. 1:12). Characterized by self-evaluation of previous stages; interests in others and their growth helps to reshape and maintain a productive purposeful life; optimistic view of one's' own spiritual capabilities, through Christ, to influence others and positively affect their lives in the name of Jesus

Success= Gains in wisdom, knowledge and expertise benefit a greater good; content and accepting of physical death as the completion of spiritual growth Failure= Focus on declining abilities; loss; despair; dogmatically holding on to a negative view of life

SUMMARY: STAIRWAY OF SPIRITUAL LIFE

Stages 1-3 — ***It Is All About Me***

- God is only seen as someone who can help me.
- My prayers consist of personal requests usually for material things

Stages 4&5 — ***It Is All About Relationship with Me***

- I am the central character in this play called life.
- A relationship with God must benefit me.
- I have increased faith in the Grace of God and His providence for me.
- I possess better primary understanding of the Holy Spirit, Christ's sacrifice for my sins which gives me righteous standing before God.
- Jesus has saved me and I have an ongoing relationship with God because of Him.

Stages 6-8 — ***It Is All About Jesus***

- My life's journey becomes profoundly more meaningful as I learn more about Jesus and His ability to cleanse, transfer power and endow me with a recognizably intimate relationship with Him, who said, "My Father, who has given *them* to Me, is greater than all; and no one is able to snatch *them* out of the Father's hand. I and the Father are One" (John 10: 29-31).

Stage 9 — ***It Is All About God's Glory***

- Glorifying God is ultimate satisfaction. This road is worth living as I see an eternal future with Him.
- My eyes are open wide, like a child seeing all things as new, for the first time.
- Finally, life is refreshing as I have learned to rest and delight in the LORD

Appendix B

Your Cliffhanger: Life's Complexities

Being religious, a traditionalist, having financial prosperity, obtaining wealth and material things, gaining knowledge and the pursuit of these may all be identified as complexities of life. It has been said that anything the average person owns, must pay for, insure, clean, repair, and traditionally or customarily do are included as life's complexities.

A. Our life in the physical (flesh)

What are some of life's complexities?

Number beginning with the most important:

- Which gets your attention first?
- Which dominates your thoughts and actions?
- Which brings about worry, anxiety, and anticipation?

B. Stairway of Life stages (Spiritual)

Where are you on this stairway?

Look at your previous response regarding life's complexities:

- How do the two match-up?
- What do you believe that you must do to reach the next stair?

C. Balancing Life's Complexities:

Balancing takes Discipline

After you have read Balancing Life's complexities (in this section), take ten (10) minutes to write about a major "letting go" you have accomplished. How did it feel? Did you mourn? Are you over the mourning process? Have you grown from it, if so, how have you grown from this experience? Who, what, or where do you need to give up now, in order to grow?

THE NEST MUST GO . . . By FAITH . . .
. . . YOU CAN FLY!

"Letting Go"

Many offered to join Jesus as a disciple but they desired to do so without surrender. Jesus constantly told them that surrender—"letting go" was necessary. (Matt. 19:16-21, 29; Luke 9: 57-63) Discipleship is demanding. Following Jesus is a priority and requires a focused commitment. It necessitates a determined will because there will be opposition and in the midst of rejection we must trust in God. A desire to hold on to the old life makes one unworthy of discipleship. **Surrender is serious**. Galatians 2:20 states: "I have been crucified with Christ and I no longer live but Christ lives in me; and the life I now live, I live by faith in the Son of God who loved me and gave himself for me." According to Oswald Chambers, in My Utmost for His Highest, "Death means you stop being."[39] God wants you to" stop being the striving, controlling, earnest kind of Christian you have been."[40] You must have a day in your life, whether you remember the exact date or not, that marked your last day; a place where "your memory goes back with a chastened, pure and extraordinarily grateful remembrance."[41]A day you can say yes . . . I made an agreement; a covenant with God. Or maybe today is your day. Have you "been buried with Him, that just as Christ was raised from the dead, you may walk in newness of life?"[42] (Rom. 6:4) Oswald Chambers penned the words *White Funeral* to mean a passage from one stage of life to another; discarding the old life for a brand new one or jumping off the cliff and dying to previous circumstances to engage in something new. He admonishes that death must occur for the Believer followed by a "resurrection into the life of Jesus Christ."[43] God wants to take you to a place of knowing how to balance spiritual and physical choices and learn how to "let go" and unite with Him in sweet surrender.

Balancing Life's Complexities

Paul wrote: "Where the Spirit of the Lord is, there is freedom (II Corinthians 3:17) Do you know that freedom means living shrewdly and joyously? To live shrewdly we must be organized and efficient, learn to delay gratification and keep an eye on the future (Mat.10:6;

Luke 16:8). To live joyously we must live in the present rejoicing and glad, live each day to the fullest and act spontaneously when it is not destructive. To live shrewdly and joyously requires discipline. Any discipline can be difficult as you learn new behaviors and "let go" of old ones. Discipline which involves balancing life's complexities is painful because it encompasses "letting go" or giving something (maybe someone) up. Human experience, wisdom and spirituality are developed along life's mountains. Negotiating the cliffs necessitates "letting go" of something that is usually a part of ourselves such as ideologies, lifestyles, patterns of behavior, human experience, etc. While the Lord often allows the process of "letting go" to be gradual, there are times when He demands immediate action. Because our lives are not without purpose, God is *always* trying to tell us something. If we become sufficient in ourselves the complacency of preconceived notions and responsibilities entangle our lives into repetitious experiences and we stay on the cliff unable to grasp God's plan for us. "If any man be in Christ, He is a new creature; old things have passed away, behold all things have become new" (II Corinthians 5:17). We often grow to believe that the entanglement is the Lord's will. Discovering ways to balance life's complexities and to acknowledge God's call to serve demands self-knowledge, spirit searching and gathering resources that may appear extreme. Every cliffhanger brings you to the edge of confronting alternate choices. "For the weapons of our warfare are not of the flesh but have divine power to destroy strongholds. We destroy arguments and every lofty opinion raised against the knowledge of God, and take every thought captive to obey Christ, being ready to punish every disobedience; when our obedience is complete" (II Corinthians 10:4-5). As indicated by Erikson's Stages of Development, the challenge in spiritual maturity is choosing between being less involved with excessive self-centered motivations and having an impact on other people for a greater purpose. According to the Word of God, spiritual growth is achieved through the pain and suffering of the discipline needed to balance His call to serve with the complexities of life.

Think about it! Freedom means assuming total responsibility for you, while rejecting responsibility that is not truly yours. "The Lord is the Spirit, and where the Spirit of the Lord is, *there* is liberty" (II Cor.3:17).

Glossary

An aspect of being spiritual is it realigns one's sense of self to include an external component. It has been observed that even a depraved spirit will seek connection with God. It engenders the perception of an individual with the capacity to be much more than imaginable. It is an inherent tendency which is virtually instinctive, that may emerge or stay hidden according to scripts, of which humans are not conscious. However, it is when the unconscious yearning becomes known to the conscious mind that we have the choice to act upon it and worship the perceived God. In the Garden of Eden, God breathed spirit into humans, and they became living souls (Gen. 2:7). The element of the spirit, in humanity, facilitates being spiritual. Because of it we have free will and the aptitude for an intimate relationship with God; and "by this we know that we abide in Him and He in us, because He has given us of His Spirit." (I John 4:13).

Many terms are used to explain inherent human characteristics. Frequently these elements are presented as interchangeable. Here is a list with definitions of those most often misunderstood terms used as components of spirituality.

Character	Notably, who we are when no one is around. Character especially emphasizes moral and ethical qualities and is a combination of training, education, culture and values.
Disposition	Natural or acquired behavioral tendencies; a frame of mind. Aspects of behavior which are displayed over time.

Personality	What others see when they look at us. Distinctive traits of character and temperament which give a person identity.
Spiritual	The substance within humanity that recognizes the possibilities of the ephemeral; an inner longing to make life count, to search for meaning and purpose in life; is described as the consciousness of the person. Spirituality is who we are inside ourselves.
Temperament	Ways of dealing with the world demonstrated as psychological (mental, emotional and volitional) patterns. Temperament is a combination of inherent qualities established through genetics that can be nurtured and educated, but never changes.

EPILOGUE

Best We Get On With Living

As a Respiratory Therapist (RT), I loved to work in the intensive care unit, the ICU, as it is called. I enjoyed using my skills, expertise, and gifts to get people back to independent breathing. My adrenaline rushed to hear them speaking and I would say *Hallelujah!* when they were able to leave the ICU, as I remembered our journey together.

In the beginning of my career as an RT, even during routine therapy I was an instructor. I would always take time to explain how to properly take the medication, breath correctly, and even their disease process, if asked. An avid reader, I read that California had rehabilitation for people afflicted with pulmonary illness and learned all that I could about it. It came natural for me to incorporate my new skills and knowledge during my daily assignment and more natural to initiate a program. I was given the opportunity and for almost 30 years performing cardiac and pulmonary rehabilitation was how I spent my time. My coworkers would say that my job was easy as cake, easy money and choice hours. That is, every co-worker who did routine therapy (if there is such a thing). The thinking was, those employed outside of rehabilitation had to be working much harder. Why? The usual rules and prohibitions were foreign in rehab. I did not have to wear a uniform; just regular clothes and a lab coat covering them, if I chose to. And did I mention no weekends, holidays, and nightshifts? Oftentimes the perspective is that a pulmonary rehabilitation therapist treats lung disease, a cardiac nurse treats heart disease and an endocrinologist treats individuals with diabetes. So far, it does sound easy, right? As each of these specialists will attest, a person presents with multiple morbidities and just because your sign says your focus is one; it does not mean that you can ignore the other. So, my 30 years were filled with being an exercise specialist, multi-disease clinician, counselor, spiritual leader and friend. Just to name a few. I wondered why I had this passion, this unique gift; why I specifically wanted to care for people and to see them get better not just to manage a crisis. When I started and completed seminary, I was asked to consider chaplaincy, I said "No, I want to help people live! I am referring to living spiritually. There is a price to be paid to live; dying does not require much effort. Scripture offers that mankind has a tendency toward death. Death means separation. In the Bible, death is directly related to sin. Separation from God is sin. Many people are afraid to live. They are afraid of the cost; thinking that it may be too high and fearing the possibility of failure, disappointment, rejection and criticism or ridicule. I have included excerpts from a few poems and thoughts to meditate upon with the hope that you will get on with living.

Live Each Day to the Fullest
~ S. H. Payer

Be yourself . . . but be your best self.
Dare to be different and follow your own star.

When you are faced with decision,
make that decision as wisely as possible,
then forget it.

The moment of absolute certainty never arrives.
And above all, remember that God helps those
who help themselves. Act as if everything depended on you
And pray as if everything depends on God.

To live each day to the fullest has nothing to do with the amount of wealth, prospects or assets you have, want or plan to acquire. Although many people, especially the young, would disagree. It has everything to do with your state mind; the ability to take on the character of Christ (Phil 2:5). Mental state is significant in all aspects of life, particularly when deciding the state of one's being or fulfillment.

This poem says a lot when considering that cliffhanger experiences during teen and young adulthood include departed friends and loved ones, ever-changing environments, callous love, dreams deferred and a host of spiritual growth pains.

A second excerpt is from a lengthy poem written by William Wordsworth. This segment may cause one to reflect on the dawning of spiritual adulthood; the time of complete surrender:

What though the radiance which was once so bright
Be now for ever taken from my sight,
Though nothing can bring back the hour
Of splendour in the grass, of glory in the flower;
We will grieve not, rather find
Strength in what remains behind;
In the primal sympathy
Which having been must ever be;
In the soothing thoughts that spring
Out of human suffering;
In the faith that looks through death,
In years that bring the philosophic mind.

The following excerpt is a reminder of the passage in Matthew 7 which says "enter by the narrow gate, for the gate is wide and the way is easy that leads to destruction, and those who enter by it are many. For the gate is narrow and the way is hard that leads to life, and those who find it are few." Both emphasize the importance of the choices we make.

The Road Not Taken

Two roads diverged in a wood, and I-
I took the one less traveled by,
And that has made all the difference.
Robert Frost

Finally, I would like to share this poem by Assisi with the message of God which can transport your subconscious to constitute a new life (Gal. 2:20). Here are the words:

The Peace Prayer

Attributed to the 13th century Saint Francis of Assisi

Lord, make me an instrument of Thy Peace!
Where there is hatred, let me sow love.
Where there is injury, pardon.

Where there is discord, harmony.
Where there is doubt, faith.
Where there is despair, hope.
Where there is darkness, light.
Where there is sorrow, joy.

Oh Divine Master, grant that I may not
So much seek to be consoled as to console;
To be understood as to understand;
To be loved as to love;

For it is in giving that we receive;
It is in pardoning that we are pardoned;
And it is in dying that we are born to Eternal Life.

In the text, *When All You've Ever Wanted Isn't Enough,* Kushman quotes the philosopher Horace Kallen whose statement epitomizes the notion of "Best We Get On With Living!" He says:

> There are persons who shape their lives by the fear of death, and persons who shape their lives by the joy and satisfaction of life. The former live dying; the latter die living. I know that fate may stop me tomorrow, but death is an irrelevant contingency. Whenever, it comes, I intend to die living.[44]

"My ears had heard of you but now my eyes have seen you" (Job 42:5).

ACKNOWLEDGEMENTS

This book is written for every person who will find themselves at the mountain's edge with a decision to make that can and will change the way you feel, think and act. Although, no one can always be certain of the outcomes from circumstances, if we would ask in faith; believing, God will surely give us the wisdom to see the value of life's trials. But, if we choose to live focused on the mundane, we will never live our purposed spiritual life. This book is written to remind everyone:

- That the circumstances of this physical, material life are methods of spiritual affirmation calling for the recognition, acceptance and love of God.
- That spirituality is a process of bringing all aspects of life under the covering of our faith convictions.
- That choice of perception during testing and tribulation aid or inhibit development of spirituality.
- That Christian spirituality is rooted in the person, ministry and work of God through Jesus Christ.
- That we remember the faithfulness of God, the fullness of grace and the victory of appropriating faith.

William Wordsworth in his book, *The Complete Poetical Works* wrote: "If from the affliction somewhere do not grow honor which could not else have been; a faith, an elevation, and sanctity. If new strength be not given, nor old restored, the blame is ours;" not God's.[45]

NOTES

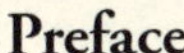

Preface

1. D. Martin. Lloyd-Jones. *Spiritual Depression*, Grand Rapids: Wm. B. Eerdmans Publishing Company, 1965. 100
2. Ibid.
3. Mary A. Fukuyama and Todd D. Sevig. *Integrating Spirituality into Multicultural Counseling,* Thousand Oaks: Sage Publications, Inc. 1998. 5-6

Chapter One

4. Thomas Carlyle. Selected Writings, *Signs of the Times,* New York: Penguin Classics, 1980.
5. Oswald Chambers. *My Utmost for His Highest*, Grand Rapids: Discovery House Publishers, 1993. July 30
6. Charles F. Pfeiffer & Everett F. Harrison. *The Wycliffe Bible Commentary*, Chicago: Moody Press, 1990. 6-8
7. Rebecca Brown, *Women on High: Pioneers of Mountaineering*, Boston: Appalachian Mountain Club Books, 2002. 225
8. Ibid.
9. D. Martin. Lloyd-Jones. *Spiritual Depression*, Grand Rapids: Wm. B. Eerdmans Publishing Company, 1965. 52
10. Ibid., 61

Chapter Two

11. Oswald Chambers, *The Complete Works of Oswald Chambers*, Grand Rapids: Discovery House Publishers, 2000. 958

12. Christine Schaub. *Finding Anna*, Minneapolis: Bethany House Books, 2005

Chapter Three

13. Henry T. Blackaby & Claude V. King. *Experiencing God*, Nashville: Broadman & Holman Publishers, 1998. 266-67
14. William McDonald. *Believer's Bible Commentary*, Nashville: Thomas Nelson Publishers, 1995. 279
15. Ibid.

Chapter Four

16. Charles Colson and Ellen Vaughn. *Gideon's Torch*, Nashville: W Pub Group, 1995.75
17. http://www.goodreads.com/author/quotes/18943. Frederick Douglass
18. Saint Augustine. *Concerning the City of God against the Pagans*, New York: Penguin Classics, 2003. Xliv
19. Samuel Terrien. The Religion of Israel. *The Interpreter's One-Volume Commentary on the Bible*, Nashville: Abingdon Press, 1980. 1158
20. Ibid.
21. Ibid.
22. Charles Spurgeon. *Being God's Friend*, New Kensington PA: Whitaker House, 1997. 18
23. W. E. Vine. *Vine's Complete Expository Dictionary*, Nashville: Thomas Nelson Publishers, 1996. 222
24. Charles Spurgeon. *Being God's Friend*, New Kensington PA: Whitaker House, 1997. 37
25. W. E. Vine. *Vine's Complete Expository Dictionary*, Nashville: Thomas Nelson Publishers, 1996. 222

Chapter Five

26. Charles Spurgeon. *Being God's Friend*, New Kensington PA: Whitaker House, 1997. 90
27. Gary Chapman, the Five Love Languages, Chicago: Northfield Publishing, 1995. 135

Chapter Six

28. "Change." Dictonary.com Unabridged. Random House, Inc. 11 September 20011. <dictionary.com http://dictionary.reference.com/browse/change>.
29. James Strong. *The New Strong's Exhaustive Concordance of the Bible,* Nashville: Thomas Nelson Publishers, 1990. 1682, 2583, 3306, 3427, 3885, 5875; USG 2
30. Oswald Chambers, *the Complete Works of Oswald Chambers*, Grand Rapids: Discovery House Publishers, 2000. 578
31. *American Heritage Dictionary.* Boston: Houghton Mifflin, Harcourt Publishing Co., 2011.
32. Henry David Thoreau. Walden. *Higher Laws*, New Haven: Yale University Press, 2004. 202

Chapter Seven

33. Ralph Earle. *Word Meanings in the New Testament*, Grand Rapids: Baker Book House, 1991.
34. David Jeremiah. Today's Turning Point, *Walk by Faith,* June 27, 2012.
35. Ibid.
36. Rebecca Brown, *Women on High: Pioneers of Mountaineering*, Boston: Appalachian Mountain Club Books, 2002. 161-162
37. Ibid. 163
38. T. D. Jakes, *Peaks and Valleys*, Shippensburg, PA: Destiny Image Publishers, 1994. 110

Appendix

39. Oswald Chambers. *My Utmost for His Highest*, Grand Rapids: Discovery House Publishers, 1993. January 15
40. Ibid.
41. Ibid.
42. Ibid.
43. Ibid.
44. Kushner, Harold. When All You've Ever Wanted Isn't Enough, New York: Simon and Schuster, Inc. 1986. 161
45. William Wordsworth. *The Complete Poetical Works*, London: Macmillan and Co., 1999. 460

Bibliography

American Heritage Dictionary, Boston: Houghton Mifflin, Harcourt Publishing Co., 2011.

Saint Augustine. *Concerning the City of God against the Pagans*, New York: Penguin Classics, 2003.

Blackaby, Henry T. & King Claude V. *Experiencing God*, Nashville: Broadman & Holman Publishers, 1998.

Brown, Rebecca. *Women on High: Pioneers of Mountaineering*, Boston: Appalachian Mountain Club Books, 2002.

Carlyle, Thomas. Selected Writings, *Signs of the Times,* New York: Penguin Classics, 1980.

Chambers, Oswald. *My Utmost for His Highest*, Grand Rapids: Discovery House Publishers, 1993. January 15, July 30

Chambers, Oswald. *The Complete Works of Oswald Chambers*, Grand Rapids: Discovery House Publishers, 2000.

"Change." Dictonary.com Unabridged. Random House, Inc. 11 September 20011. <dictionary.com http://dictionary.reference.com/browse/change>.

Chapman, Gary. *The Five Love Languages*, Chicago: Northfield Publishing, 1995.

Colson, Charles and Vaughn, Ellen. *Gideon's Torch*, Nashville: W Pub Group, 1995.

Earle, Ralph. *Word Meanings in the New Testament*, Grand Rapids: Baker Book House, 1991.

Frost, Robert. *The Poetry of Robert Frost*, ed. Edward Connery Lathem, New York: Holt, Rinehart and Winston, 1969.

Fukuyama, Mary A. and Sevig, Todd D. *Integrating Spirituality into Multicultural Counseling*, Thousand Oaks: Sage Publications, Inc. 1998.

http://www.goodreads.com/author/quotes/18943.Frederick_Douglass

Jakes, T. D. *Peaks and Valleys*, Shippensburg, PA: Destiny Image Publishers, 1994.

Jeremiah, David. Today's Turning Point, *Walk by Faith,* June 27, 2012.

Kushman, Harold. *When All You've Ever Wanted Isn't Enough*, New York: Simon and Schuster, Inc., 1986.

Lloyd-Jones, D. Martin. *Spiritual Depression*, Grand Rapids: Wm. B.Eerdmans Publishing Company, 1965.

McDonald, William. *Believer's Bible Commentary*, Nashville: Thomas Nelson Publishers, 1995.

Payer, S. H. *Live Each Day to the Fullest*, Brooklyn OH: American Greetings, 1970.

Peck, M. Scott. *The Road Less Traveled*, New York: Simon and Schuster Publishers, 2003.

Pfeiffer, Charles F. & Harrison, Everett F. *The Wycliffe Bible Commentary*, Chicago: Moody Press, 1990.

Proctor, Adelaide A. *The Poems of Adelaide A. Procter*, Boston: James R. Osgood & Company, 1872.

Schaub, Christine. *Finding Anna*, Minneapolis: Bethany House Books, 2005

Shirer, Priscilla. *A Jewel in His Crown*, Chicago: Moody Publishers, 1999.

Strong, James. *The New Strong's Exhaustive Concordance of the Bible*, Nashville: Thomas Nelson Publishers, 1990.

Spurgeon, Charles. *Being God's Friend,* New Kensington: Whitaker House, 1997.

Terrien, Samuel. The Religion of Israel. *The Interpreter's One Volume Commentary on the Bible*, Nashville: Abingdon Press, 1980.

Thoreau, Henry David. Walden. *Higher Laws*, New Haven: Yale University Press, 2004

Vine, W. E. *Vine's Complete Expository Dictionary*, Nashville: Thomas Nelson Publishers, 1996.

Wordsworth, William. *The Complete Poetical Works*, London: Macmillan and Co., 1999.

Printed in the United States
By Bookmasters